PUPPY
PARENTING

PUPPY PARENTING

AN EXPERT GUIDE ON WHAT TO DO
AND WHEN TO DO IT

Dr Scott Miller

Bounty
Books

First published in Great Britain in 2007 by Hamlyn,
a division of Octopus Publishing Group Ltd.

This edition published in 2011 by Bounty Books,
a division of Octopus Publishing Group Ltd,
Endeavour House, 189 Shaftesbury Avenue,
London WC2H 8JY
www.octopusbooks.co.uk

An Hachette UK Company
www.hachette.co.uk

ISBN: 978-0-753721-37-7

A CIP catalogue record for this book is
available from the British Library

Printed and bound in China

The advice in this book is provided as general information only.
It is not necessarily specific to any individual case and is not a
substitute for the guidance and advice provided by a licensed
veterinary practitioner consulted in any particular situation.
Octopus Publishing Group accepts no liability or responsibility
for any consequences resulting from the use of or reliance
upon the information contained herein.

No dogs or puppies were harmed in the making of this book.

Unless the information given in this book is specifically for
female dogs, dogs are referred to throughout as 'he'. The
information is equally applicable to both male and female
dogs, unless otherwise specified.

Contents

Introduction

After a few barren years without a dog in my life, Betty burst onto the scene, bringing carnage, exuberance and, most of all, joy. Watching her grow has been a delight and has taught me so much about being both a vet and a puppy parent.

The lessons learned and the experience gained on this rewarding and at times testing journey through Betty's puppyhood have inspired me to write this book. I hope that it will enlighten not dictate and encourage rather than daunt, by offering simple, practical advice and a month-by-month guide to what you should expect as your puppy grows. At intervals throughout the book, this guidance is complemented by entries from Betty's Diary that provide illuminating episodes from my personal experience. They prove that all of us (even a vet!) can make mistakes, but that we can all learn from these, building our patience and understanding to become good puppy parents. Throughout the book you'll also find answers to all the questions often asked about bringing up a puppy, as well as explanations of 'old wives' tails' – the stories about dogs that are sometimes far from the truth.

PERFECT PUPPY PARTNER

With over 5 million dogs owned in the UK and 73 million in the USA, canine companions are as popular as ever. From the microscopic Chihuahua to the Giant Schnauzer, dogs come in many shapes and sizes to suit their different owners. Short coat or long, affectionate or self-reliant, apartment dwellers or farm animals, dogs have been bred into such varying forms that they can match almost any individual owner's requirements.

But why do we feel the need to have a dog in the first place? Dogs make noise, take up valuable relaxation time, shed fur and of course eat you out of house and home. The answer is simple – because they give us unconditional love. Dogs provide us with a topic of conversation, a reason to venture out of the house and an abundance of joy. They also afford us companionship and protection, and strengthen the family unit by providing a source of humour, a common interest and an outlet for our affection.

It is well documented that the presence of a dog in home and office environments decreases stress and improves the outlook of those suffering from depression. Canine companions also help foster personal responsibility and understanding of animals in children, as well as encouraging us all to exercise and teaching us how to share. From puppyhood and throughout their lives dogs maintain a child-like quality that brings out the nurturing side in their human friends, ensuring that our affection for them never diminishes.

Any parent will tell you that to be forewarned is to be forearmed, and puppy parenting is no different. Few events will change your life more dramatically than owning a dog. The advice in this book will fully prepare you for your new parental role, ensuring that your puppy grows into a well-adjusted, healthy and loyal companion that will shower you with love to last a lifetime.

Dr Scott

▶ The bond of love between Betty and I continues to grow, giving us daily reasons to jump for joy.

The potential puppy parent

Initial questions

Dog ownership requires a great deal of consideration – the impulse purchase of a little ball of fur can end in disaster for both you and him. Your environment, bank balance, personality, human and animal house-mates and spare time are all crucial elements to take into account. This chapter will steer you towards making the right choice of puppy, ensuring a match made in heaven.

SHOULD I OWN A DOG?
Consider carefully

Puppies are undeniably enchanting, though however wonderful they are they remain a huge undertaking and the decision to own one should not be entered into lightly. As a potential future life partner, a canine should not be a fashionable or spur-of the-moment purchase and many factors must be addressed before a dog is brought into your home. If picking up faeces, clearing up dog hair, having your shoes chewed and going out for walks in all weathers doesn't appeal, then you need not apply for the job of dog owner. But if you have taken all the onerous duties into account and made the decision wisely, choosing to share your life with a dog can lead to one of the most beneficial, enduring and loving relationships that a human being can experience.

Pros
- Unconditional love
- Companionship
- Improved general physical health
- Fostering of responsibility in children
- Increased interest in the outdoors
- Opportunity to meet other dog owners
- Decreased stress levels and help in coping with depression

Cons
- Responsibility
- Cost
- Time

WHAT SORT OF DOG IS RIGHT FOR ME?
Assess your situation

Dogs live for 12 years on average, so the onus is on you as the potential owner to consider carefully your personal circumstances in relation to all the aspects of care that different breeds or types of dog require before choosing and purchasing or re-homing a canine. The key aspects that you need to assess are your living environment, your energy levels and the amount of time and money that you have available to spend on a dog.

▲ Before shaking paws with a new canine companion, do as much research as possible to find the breed that's right for you.

SUITING YOUR CIRCUMSTANCES
Your environment

Consider the amount of space you have and relate that to the size of dog. For instance, a one-bedroom flat is an inadequate abode for an Irish Wolfhound and a country house with plenty of land may be wasted on a Maltese Terrier.

Your energy level

This is unlikely to change significantly with a new canine companion, so be honest about your exercise levels and choose accordingly. A Border Collie is highly energetic and intelligent, so purchasing one to keep you company while you watch television will end in tears. Conversely, if you want to spend lots of time enjoying the great outdoors, a Shih Tzu will be likely to leave you to do so on your own.

Your cash flow

There is no doubt that a dog is expensive, requiring on-going nutrition and veterinary treatment at the bare minimum. Larger dogs are sure to cost more in food bills alone, so factor this into your decision.

Your time

Some breeds are less time-consuming than others in terms of grooming or exercise requirements. But any dog will take up on average two to three hours per day of your time, and can be left alone for four hours at the very most. Any pet requires care and attention, so if you don't have the time, don't get one.

Potential owner
RÉSUMÉ

Name: A N Owner

Age Adult enough to appreciate the lifelong commitment entered into when getting a dog.

Sex Either sex will enjoy the companionship that a dog can bring.

Height and weight These factors need play little part in which puppy you choose, as long as it is well trained.

Marital and family status The more the merrier; a puppy is a big undertaking for a single owner on a fixed working schedule. Partners and children help to share the burden and the rewards.

Nationality All nations of the world are home to dogs and dog owners.

Education A basic appreciation of general care is all that is needed; much of the learning about a puppy's upbringing is completed 'on the job'.

Occupation Any that allows adequate time to be spent with your new puppy without long periods when he is left on his own.

Activity level Whatever it is currently will increase once a dog is purchased.

Personality traits Patient, responsible, trustworthy, loving, hard-working, dedicated, understanding and kind.

Medical complaints Some dogs may have a characteristic that exacerbates a particular condition; excessive moulting, for example, could worsen symptoms of asthma. However, dogs can also help their owners deal with certain complaints. For example, having a dog can aid recovery from illness and combat feelings of loneliness and isolation.

Other interests If you enjoy maintaining a healthy lifestyle and outdoor pursuits, such as walking and exploring the countryside, your pleasure will only be increased with a well-behaved canine at your side.

Potential puppy
RÉSUMÉ

Name: K-9

Age 8 weeks. I can live from 8–18 years, the average being 12–14 years.

Sex Males and females may vary in size and temperament.

Height and weight Varies from 7–102 cm (3–40 in) in height; 1–100 kg (2–220 lb) in weight.

Marital and family status Single and looking for love and companionship.

Nationality Originally from the Northern hemisphere, presumably the Middle East, there are hundreds of dog breeds in existence from many nations.

Education Up to you – I am open to suggestions.

Occupation Potential for skill in hunting, protection, sports and specialist fields (examples of the latter include sniffer, hearing and guide dogs).

Activity level High as a puppy, then can be estimated according to the average activity level of my breed.

Personality traits Loyal, affectionate and honest. Other personality strengths can come from the parents and breed.

Medical complaints From none to many, depending on the individual and breed-specific illnesses.

Other interests Anything that interests you!

BETTY'S DIARY
visions of you

I had contemplated getting another dog for a long time, but was only just beginning to feel ready after having lost my previous dog, a rescue English Bull Terrier called Zed, two years previously. Although Zed had suffered at the hands of his former, neglectful owners, he regained full health to become one of the sweetest and kind-natured dogs imaginable. Good with other dogs and children, he did his much-maligned breed proud and when he died my whole family and I were deeply saddened.

I found it difficult to contemplate another dog being more special than my Zed, but eventually came round to the possibility of bringing another canine into my home. For the first time in my life I decided on a puppy, as opposed to re-homing more mature rescue pets as I had done in the past. I also decided to get a female dog, just to complete the contrast with my previous male dog Zed. As I was living in inner-city London and my outside space

was limited to a decent-sized terrace, I decided to choose a smaller dog. I also thought it would be a good idea to get one with short hair, as grooming is not my strong suit.

As a vet, I am exposed to the wonderful array of dog breeds brought into the clinic, caring for them at their worst during times of stress, fear or pain. I had always found Border Terriers exemplary patients, accepting treatment and afterwards giving a lick on the face as a thank you. They are relatively energetic dogs but also enjoy lazing around the house – a mixture that seemed perfect. I am quite an active guy so I liked the idea that a trained terrier would be sociable with all types of people and dogs, enjoy runs and be entertaining in the park.

Although very busy with my work, I rationalized that I would be able to take my new charge to the clinic and the television studio and spend long periods at home with her, so I had the necessary time to dedicate to a canine companion. I was also in a financial position to support a dog, and my job meant that vet bills would be minimized! And so my search to buy a female Border Terrier puppy began . . .

SHOULD I CHOOSE A PURE BREED OR CROSSBREED?

Do your research

If you buy a pure-bred dog, you know what you are getting. That said, pedigree dogs are known to suffer more than crossbreeds from inherited diseases due to inbreeding (see page 20). Research the different breeds and thoroughly question breeders before choosing a puppy. Search for top-quality breeders using reputable dog clubs such as your national Kennel Club, which lists breeders and where to find them. Consider visiting local dog shows before you choose a potential pedigree partner in order to see which canine takes your fancy.

Crossbreeds are in general terms no better or worse as pets, companions, working dogs or competitors in dog sports than pure-bred dogs and they have fewer inherited health problems. However, such dogs are often the result of unplanned pregnancies, so care of the litter can sometimes be lacking. Always meet the parents of the puppy before purchase to gauge its potential size and temperament when fully grown.

While meeting the parents may not be possible if you decide to re-home a crossbreed or mongrel from a welfare centre (see page 13), you will be doing the community a service and may rescue an unwanted dog that might otherwise be destroyed.

IS A DOG PREFERABLE TO A BITCH?

Take your pick

There is little variability between the sexes to be observed in smaller dogs, but in bigger dogs the differences are more obvious. Male dogs can be more confident and outgoing, but they can also be more aggressive to other dogs. Bitches are generally more agreeable in temperament, although this can fluctuate during times of season (averaging twice a year) if not spayed. For the purposes of choosing a pet, experience as a vet has proven to me that gender is not a decisive issue. When dogs are neutered (see page 110), there is little difference between the sexes and both make equally wonderful pets.

▲ From the comical to the startling, crossbreeds can come in all shapes and sizes.

SHOULD I BUY FROM A PET SHOP OR PRIVATELY?

Breeders are best

Pet shops vary greatly in quality of service and in the standard of health of the puppies they sell. If you choose to use a pet shop, visit first and assure yourself that the puppy facilities are spotless and the proprietor's knowledge and standards of practice are acceptable.

Buying from individual breeders or homes allows you to see where the puppy comes from and gives you the chance to meet and inspect the parents at first hand. Breeders tend to have an honest interest in ensuring that their puppies go to good homes and are likely to give free post-purchase advice. While most breeders home puppies only after they have had their first set of vaccinations and health checks, always seek the advice of a vet before purchasing a puppy.

SHOULD I CONSIDER GETTING A PUPPY FROM A WELFARE CENTRE?

Pros and cons

If you choose a puppy from a welfare centre, you will be giving a home to an unwanted animal and potentially saving a life. Also, the donation you give to the centre, normally part of the transaction, will fund the care of other homeless animals. On the downside, the puppy's potential adult size and temperament may be difficult to determine and his medical history may be unknown.

WHICH BREED SHOULD I CHOOSE?

Match your personality

Today's dogs come in all shapes and sizes, with over 200 breeds recognized throughout the world. Pure-bred dogs are categorized in seven main

▼ Choosing a breed can be easier than picking out one puppy from a litter.

groupings: gundog, hound, pastoral, terrier, toy, utility and working. Then, of course, there is the ever-present and lovable mongrel, which may also be given the names 'mixed-breed', 'mutt' and 'bitsa' (as in bits of this and bits of that!). These dogs all belong to the same species, *Canis familiaris*, which means that any two breeds can inter-mate and produce fertile offspring – even in the case of an unlikely pairing between a Great Dane and a Chihuahua!

The breed groups are defined mainly by temperament and range from the intelligent and sociable gundogs, who often make great family pets, to the physically imposing working dogs, who need a strong hand and lots of space. Choosing a breed of dog could start with selecting a group that best matches your personality and lifestyle, then narrowing down your choice from there. Breed groupings vary slightly between countries, but the common characteristics for each group are presented on the following pages.

▲ Golden Retriever

Hound

Also hunting dogs, hounds would run to catch and hold prey, such as badgers, hares or deer, until their owners arrived on foot or horseback. This behaviour can be translated into non-hunting environments, meaning these canines may chase wildlife in the park or small animals, including cats, at home.

Occasional disobedience and strong will are only minor drawbacks to these highly sociable and friendly dogs. Members of this group are known for their gentle affection towards children and amicable nature when meeting other dogs. Ideal for an active family who enjoy energetic daily walks, they also happily relax at home. Sedentary, overweight hounds may suffer spinal problems as a result of the strain that excess weight puts on their elongated backs.

Most popular members include: Dachshund, Beagle, Whippet, Basset Hound, Greyhound, Afghan Hound.

THE BREED GROUPS

Gundog

Bred to flush and retrieve game, this sporting group traditionally popular with the shooting fraternity represents many of the pet canines found in the households of today. Generally medium- to large-sized dogs, the puppies are often highly intelligent and sociable, resulting in an easily trained, affable pet. The oral dexterity demanded by these dogs' historic profession can equate to insatiable chewing in their modern stay-at-home counterparts. The problem can be overcome by supplying them with an interesting array of toys, for which they have a near obsession.

Their boundless capacity for exercise and play is only overtaken by their love of food, so a balance between the two is needed to ensure a healthy and trim dog. These fun-loving and friendly canines enjoy a close bond with their owners and are great pets for children and adults alike. Generally easy to look after, gundogs enjoy nothing more than a long walk and plenty of affection.

Most popular members include: Labrador, Golden Retriever, Cocker Spaniel, English Springer Spaniel, Weimaraner, Irish Setter.

▲ Dachshund

Pastoral

Somewhat ambiguously named, the pastoral group (classified as the herding group in the USA) consists of dogs that are bred to work with domesticated mammals that graze on pastures. These are divided into two subgroupings: herding dogs that round up flocks of sheep, herds of cattle or even reindeer under the direction of their owners, and protecting dogs that were bred to live with and look after flocks of sheep.

Herding Dogs in this subgroup are renowned for their agility, activity and intellect. They are easily

▲ German Shepherd Dog

Protecting The dogs in this pastoral subgroup are known to patrol the house and guard the family. These animals are larger and more powerfully built to enable them to fight off predators and they can be prone to aggression with other dogs and people if they are not adequately socialized. They have also developed a heavier coat to withstand the cold temperatures to which they were traditionally exposed to while watching over the sheep or reindeer at night. Tending to be a little stronger willed, they can be quite stubborn and less energetic than their herding cousins.

Most popular members include: Samoyed, Bergamasco, Komondor, Pyrenean Mountain Dog.

trained, reliable and obedient. Many suffer with behavioural problems if not adequately stimulated and require a large amount of exercise if kept in a suburban environment. They have ultra-keen senses, so can be prone to noise phobia or general nervousness unless exposed to traffic and plenty of people as puppies. Their personality traits make them particularly suitable for use in professions such as the police service and they also make excellent candidates for agility competitions.

Most popular members include: Corgi, Border Collie, Bearded Collie, German Shepherd Dog, Old English Sheepdog.

▲ Samoyed

Toy

Breeds without any specific active purpose, these canines are regarded as companions. Usually small in stature, they are easily trained and very agreeable, enjoying play and entertaining their owners. Since they are small dogs, they can be frightened of children and other dogs. They are also easy to spoil and thus are prone to obesity. Not being particularly active dogs, these canines are disinclined to take long walks, preferring lots of fuss and attention from their devoted owners.

Most popular members include: Chihuahua, Cavalier King Charles Spaniel, Bichon Frise, Pug.

▲ Cavalier King Charles Spaniel

◀ Jack Russell Terrier

Terrier

Known for their energetic and independent nature, terriers were originally bred to catch and kill small mammals considered to be vermin. Foxes, badgers, rats and rabbits would fall victim to these tenacious and feisty canines, which carry the instinct to hunt and kill into the home environment. Given that they like to give chase and bite hard, terriers can pose a threat to cats and other small mammals if they do not have exposure to them as puppies. Yet terriers remain one of the most popular groups of canine pet, with strong protective instincts, energetic personalities and the ability to entertain themselves at home with toys.

A good daily walk is all that is needed for most terriers as long as they are supplied with games and suitable toys, with which they will run around the house. Tending to be a vocal group of dogs, terriers can be regarded as either good watchdogs or rather noisy, depending on the circumstances, and are variable in behaviour towards other dogs.

Most popular members include: Jack Russell Terrier, Fox Terrier, West Highland White Terrier, Staffordshire Bull Terrier, Bull Terrier.

Utility

Otherwise known as the non-sporting group, this category encompasses a mixture of dogs that have been bred to undertake a variety of tasks, generally other than hunting, within human society. As a result, these breeds come in all manner of shapes, coats and sizes. Excelling in herding and guarding, many individuals within the group have shown exceptional bravery and valour in their protective roles towards humans. As utility dogs vary greatly in temperament, owners usually choose a type on the basis of appearance and then research each breed's specific traits.

Most popular members include: Shih Tzu, Bulldog, Dalmatian, Poodle and Schnauzer.

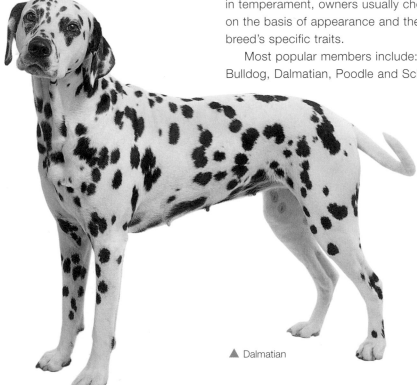

▲ Dalmatian

Working

Usually bred as guard dogs, these are large to extra-large dogs with great physical presence. They are also used in specialized search and rescue fields. Requiring moderate exercise and plenty of food, these big dogs need a lot of space and a big budget. They are very loyal to their owners, but strict leadership is needed from the outset of buying a puppy to ensure that you are fully in control of these strong beasts into adulthood. These giants of the dog world tend to be the shortest lived of all breed groups.

Although generally having shorter fur and therefore minimal grooming requirements, working dogs demand more specialist care and ownership than other breeds. A big responsibility in more ways than one, working breeds are not recommended for the first-time dog owner.

Most popular members include: Boxer, Dobermann, Rottweiler, Great Dane, St Bernard and Bullmastiff.

▲ Great Dane

Crossbreeds

Many dogs are a combination of two of more breeds, resulting in offspring that can vary greatly in size, appearance and personality. As a result of mixed parentage, these dogs tend to avoid many of the inherited diseases seen in pure-bred dogs.

With much greater variability within the gene pool, a cross-bred puppy can undergo significant change as it develops to grow into a dog on a scale that you hadn't expected. The temperament and strength of crossbreeds are also variable. Given responsible ownership and love these dogs can make just as good companions as their shorter-lived, pure-bred counterparts.

If cross-bred puppies are acquired from a local welfare centre or dog home, you are doubling your achievement as you are giving a home to a puppy that desperately needs one at the same time as gaining a new life partner.

Most popular types include: Labradoodle, Cockerpoo, Puggle, mongrel (no definable type or breed).

▶ Jack Russell–Border Terrier crossbreed

HOW DO I FIND A PUPPY?
Select your source
Once you have identified a breed of dog that fits your personality and lifestyle, the next step is to find a litter of puppies. There are many ways to source a breeder or welfare centre, via the internet, library, phone directory, newspapers, magazines or word of mouth. Dog shows also offer the opportunity to learn more about your chosen breed, obtain contact details of local breeders and find out when puppies may be due. Many countries worldwide have their own national Kennel Club – a respected organization that offers an ideal starting point for gaining information about breeders and dog breeds alike.

Be prepared
It is always a good idea to have a basic knowledge of dogs and your specific breed before you begin searching for puppies. This information will help you to distinguish between respectable breeders or welfare centres and pretenders.

▲ To find the perfect puppy, check out dog shows, websites or magazines, and talk to the Kennel Club or local dog shelters.

Be discerning
If you find the breeders or vendors to be unfriendly, unhelpful or not particularly knowledgeable, take your leave. Honest breeders will openly discuss the negative attributes of their breed along with the positive ones, as they will want their puppies to go to suitable homes and not just anyone with the right purchase price in their pocket.

Much of a puppy's behaviour comes from his parents and socialization with humans in the early stages of life, so if you don't like the sound of a breeder it's possible that some of that less-than-desirable personality may rub off on the puppy. If you are at all concerned regarding a breeder's credibility, it is best to take your custom elsewhere. In any case, it is advisable not to buy a puppy on first viewing, but to allow yourself the necessary time and space to consider the purchase without feeling pressured.

Look for cleanliness

General hygiene should always be highly regarded. Puppies who have been living in squalid conditions and who have been exposed to disease are more likely to suffer from a weakened immune system into adulthood. Before you even consider buying a puppy, check out the cleanliness of the establishment. If it doesn't match your high expectations, you should take your search for a healthy puppy elsewhere.

What to ask the breeder

About the parents Always ask to meet the parents of puppies so that you are aware of the size of dog that your puppy will eventually become. The personality of your puppy can also be gauged by his parents, so if both parents are friendly and easy-going then you can assume that their puppies will be similarly tempered. If the breeder is unable to show you the parents, be very dubious of the sale. Beware of puppy farms, where bitches are constantly bred without their health being taken into account, producing as many puppies as possible for the pet trade. Parent dogs kept in such circumstances will be thin and in poor condition generally, so are likely to be kept away from any prospective new owners.

About vaccination and worming Always ask about the details of the puppy's vaccination and worming history and make sure you obtain written evidence from the breeder signed by a vet. All puppies should have been vaccinated once prior to sale and have had at least one worming treatment as a bare minimum. If this has not been done, again be dubious of the sale and don't commit.

About illnesses and inherited diseases Ask if there are any known illnesses in the puppy's family or breed. If your choice of breed is known to be at risk from suffering inherited disease (see page 20), discuss this from the outset with the breeder and ask to see reports confirming the puppy's parents' genetic health. This could include X-ray reports of hip scoring and DNA or blood test results, which should confirm that the parents of your puppy are fit to breed.

▼ Meet the parents: playful, friendly and happy parents tend to produce similarly natured puppies.

PAWS FOR THOUGHT
inherited diseases

Pure-bred dogs by definition have required some inbreeding during the development of the breed in order to attain a particular set of characteristics. With intensive breeding, physical traits such as coat appearance and body structure have been fine-tuned and passed on to offspring via genetic information stored in DNA. The concentration of these positive traits has also accumulated inherited diseases, passed on genetically from parent to offspring. Commonly noted inherited defects include heart murmurs in Cavalier King Charles Spaniels, degenerative joint disease in German Shepherd Dogs and skin disease in Shar Peis.

Today, respectable breeders do their utmost to ensure that puppies produced by them shed the negative genetic attributes of their breed by mating only those dogs free of inherited conditions. Be aware of any known genetic disorders carried by your breed of choice, discussing these fully with your vet and breeder before purchasing a new puppy. Finding out about these conditions will help you to choose a healthy puppy and avoid inheriting your own set of problems, both financial and emotional.

WHAT IF I HAVE A CAT?
Consider your feline's personality

Think carefully about the personality of your cat before contemplating a dog, as a cat of a nervous disposition may totally reject the idea of a canine companion, choosing to vacate your house or injure the new arrival. In any event, there will be troubled times ahead, with extra work and attention needing to be given to both animals to help ease the situation. Most cats will not appreciate the new smells and sounds or the unwanted attentions of the puppy and may lash out aggressively or hide away in the early stages of introduction.

Avoid inappropriate breeds

Some dog breeds have strong hunting instincts (see page 14), so this should be considered when choosing a puppy to enter a home containing a resident feline or other smaller pets.

WHAT IF I HAVE ANOTHER DOG?
Counteract jealousy

As dogs are pack animals, most will enjoy the company of another member of their species and will welcome the attention offered by a puppy. It may take a few days for your older dog to come to terms with the new arrival, however, so make sure that you lavish more affection on him than you did before the puppy arrived to avoid jealousy.

Proceed with care

Dogs are aware of the relative age of a puppy, but do not allow yourself to lapse into a false sense of security and expect that your current canine companion will naturally accept your new arrival with ease. You will need to introduce them in a controlled way and oversee their interactions for the first few weeks.

Know when to say no

You should have a good idea of how your existing dog behaves with other dogs, and if after honest

◀ A healthy confident puppy, whether it is pure-bred or cross-bred, should enjoy the outdoors in all weathers.

reflection you conclude that he is stalwartly antisocial in nature, acquiring a puppy may not be an appropriate move in the circumstances.

WHAT IF I HAVE CHILDREN?

Choose an appropriate breed

Most puppies enjoy the company of children, who are generally smaller and less frightening than the much larger adult humans. Certain dog breeds are known for their excellent temperament around children, but other breeds with strong prey instincts may be more unpredictable.

Research the breeds of dog that you are considering in terms of their behaviour around children, asking the breeder for advice regarding this important character trait. If you have very small children in your home, it is paramount that you choose a dog that has a genetic predisposition to good behaviour with children and take into consideration the size of the grown dog in relation to your growing family.

In any case, at no stage in your chosen puppy's development should you trust him to be alone with children – always chaperone interactions to ensure safety for all involved and teach children how to behave correctly with him.

▶ If you have children in your home, consider a friendly breed such as a Golden Retriever.

Child-friendly breeds	Breeds to avoid around children
Airedale Terrier	Affenpinscher
Cairn Terrier	Chihuahua
Cavalier King Charles Spaniel	Chow Chow
Golden Retriever	Dobermann
Labrador	German Shepherd Dog
Newfoundland	Hungarian Puli
Poodle	Pit Bull Terrier
Pug	Rottweiler
Schnauzer	Saluki
Whippet	Weimaraner

HOW DO I CHOOSE A PUPPY?
Make an informed choice
Choosing a well-balanced, healthy puppy is not as easy as it seems. Forearm yourself with some basic knowledge to complement your common sense. Be sensible in your choice – don't let guilt lead you to choose a weak, ill or nervous puppy. A poor health record as a puppy can lead to a weakened immune system and other health issues as an adult, resulting in financial and emotional burdens that may be hard to cope with. Such an individual is best kept in the capable hands of the breeder and his mum. Always reserve the right to say no.

Temperament indicators
The puppy you choose should be alert and interested in you, without showing overt signs of aggression. The opposite extreme is not a good choice either – a fearful puppy indicates either inherent nervousness or poor socialization of the puppies by the vendor.

What to look for
Pick up the puppy and he should feel heavier than you expect; a light or thin puppy could indicate ill health. He should be relaxed in your grasp and when released interact well with you and his littermates, giving an indication of the type of dog he will become. You should also carry out a basic health check (see opposite).

WHEN SHOULD I TAKE THE PUPPY HOME?
Optimum age
Your puppy should be at least eight weeks of age. Any younger and he may be too weak or improperly weaned to be torn away from his mum. At eight weeks puppies are at the optimum developmental stage to leave their littermates and begin life in a new home. They have developed enough canine social and play skills by being with their siblings and mother and now need to understand humans and how to relate to their world.

◀ Any excuse for a cuddle – pick up the puppy to check his weight and temperament.

BASIC HEALTH CHECK

Eyes These should be bright and fully open, with no discharge or redness, as this can indicate disease.

Gums These should be pink, indicating that the puppy is healthy and not anaemic from worms or ill health.

Genitals and anus Males should have two testicles descended; if not, the puppy is classified as cryptorchid and requires surgical treatment to correct the condition. Females should have a clean vulva. Both sexes should be checked for any diarrhoea staining around the anus, which could indicate gut upsets, worms or early digestive problems.

Ears Check that there is no wax build-up in the ear canals and no smell evident, which could indicate infection. Check the pinnae (ear flaps) for skin disease.

Skin and coat A shiny coat free of dandruff indicates a healthy dog. Patches of hair loss and scabbing lesions could indicate fungal infection or external parasite infestation.

Umbilicus (belly button) Check that this is flat; a swelling near this site can indicate hernia and may need surgical correction.

Feet and nails Dogs have five toes on the front feet and generally four on the back, occasionally with a dewclaw (the functionless remnant of a big toe) on the inside of the hind leg. All nails should be intact and unbroken.

To find out more on ...

Anaemia, go to page 140
Conversing in canine, go to page 49
Flea control, go to page 42
Meeting cats, go to page 56
Meeting children, go to page 58
Meeting other dogs, go to page 57
Neutering, go to page 110
Tick, lice and mite control, go to page 42
Vaccinations, go to page 39
Worming, go to page 40

Preparing for parenthood

Before your puppy arrives

Once you have chosen your puppy, or even before, you will need to make changes to your home environment and assemble various items of equipment in preparation for the new arrival – yes, it's just like having a baby! This is also a good time to survey the bewildering range of canine feeding options on offer.

PUPPY PARAPHERNALIA

Think ahead

It is important to consider all the wants and needs of your new puppy before he arrives on your doorstep. From where he will sleep to what he will play with, your puppy needs a lot of equipment to keep him healthy and happy. The following is a rundown of the required basics.

Food and water bowls

Plastic, stainless steel or ceramic, dog bowls come in many shapes and sizes and are a good idea to ensure a hygienic household. Plastic bowls should have a wide rim and stopper pads beneath to avoid sliding, although be mindful that the puppy may chew on more than just the food. It is essential to have at least two bowls, one for food and one for water. Fresh water should be available to your puppy at all times, so put his water bowl in a place where it won't be knocked over.

Toys

Toys are an important tool in the war against puppy chewing. They also stimulate your dog's interest in play and in investigating his environment. There is a huge array of puppy toys on the market. Be selective and choose ones that are non-toxic and have no detachable parts or sharp edges. Rubber toys are an excellent choice as they have an appealing texture and are different from other materials that your puppy may wish to chew in your home, such as shoes and furniture.

It is a good idea to have a few different toys to offer the puppy at various times of the day to avoid boredom, and this also serves to find out which he enjoys best. Regularly check toys for damage and provide new ones to keep your puppy both safe and stimulated.

Crates, play pens and bedding

The easiest way of setting up your puppy's bedroom is using a puppy crate or play pen. Usually of stainless steel construction, these foldable cages are large enough for your puppy both to play and sleep in comfortably. A puppy crate is smaller and includes a roof and a floor, while a play pen simply fences off a larger area. A play pen will allow the puppy to be contained out of harm's way during the day, enabling you to carry out household chores in peace. It will also provide the puppy with a secure sleeping enclosure at night. Place the crate or pen in a room where people frequently pass through, such as the kitchen, to make sure that the puppy does not feel excluded from the activities of the home.

A basic puppy enclosure should contain bedding in the form of blankets or a vet bed (purpose-designed animal bedding used in vet clinics and obtained from most pet retailers), an absorbent puppy training pad, a water bowl and toys. As an extra comfort for your new puppy, it is a good idea to add a blanket that carries mum's scent (see page 45), either laid on top of the bedding or vet bed or crumpled into a corner for the puppy to nuzzle.

Baskets or boxes

If you decide on giving your puppy the run of the house, hard plastic, cloth or wicker baskets are available. Bear in mind that your puppy will get bigger, so either choose a basket large enough for an adult specimen of your puppy's breed or use a temporary cardboard box until the puppy has grown. Place the bed somewhere warm and out of draughts, remembering to add a blanket with mum's scent.

▼ A range of different toys are available to suit your dog's mouth size.

Baby gate

This is a very useful purchase to help control an adventurous puppy as he grows. It can prevent accidents in the kitchen and elsewhere, stop the puppy from going out the front door or up the stairs and confine him to certain parts of the home.

Collars and leads

It is worthwhile investing in a collar and lead from day one to get your puppy acclimatized to them. Wearing a collar and attaching the lead from time to time indoors prepares your puppy for the big outside world that awaits him when his vaccination course has been completed.

It is recommended that you purchase an identity tag to place on your puppy's collar with your contact details in case he goes missing. In some countries, this is required by law.

Collars Available in a wide variety of colours, a collar should be chosen for its suitability for your puppy and not its appearance. A collar should be lightweight, with no sharp edges, and loose

enough to place at least two fingers between the collar and your puppy's neck. Check the fit before securing it around your puppy's neck and use for short but increasing periods each day. Remember to loosen the collar as your puppy grows.

Halters and harnesses You can consider using halters and harnesses later on in your dog's life when certain training methods may dictate their use. A halter may be needed if your puppy pulls excessively, or a harness may be required if he pulls out of a collar and needs something more sturdy. Chiefly made of strong nylon, harnesses avoid pressure around the neck and can be used in place of a collar. Choke chains are potentially life threatening and should not be used. Such archaic methods of control are in any case unnecessary if you are patient and a consistent training regime is implemented early on.

Leads These are available in rope, leather, chain, nylon or a mixture of materials. It is useful to have both a short and a long lead to keep your puppy in check – the shorter lead is suitable for initial indoor use, while longer extendible varieties are ideal when the puppy is allowed more freedom outdoors in the appropriate circumstances.

Grooming equipment

You will need a brush or comb to maintain your puppy's appearance, whatever his breed. Each breed has different grooming needs, so ask the breeders what they use to groom their adult dogs. Getting your puppy used to being brushed early is important if regular visits to the grooming parlour are required in the future.

Nail clippers are used by many dog owners to avoid scratches from sharp-nailed puppies. However, given that blood vessels are present in your puppy's nails, it is advisable to have a lesson from your vet or groomer before attempting nail clipping at home.

◀ Ask the breeder to advise which grooming implements are suitable for your dog's coat.

THE FOOD YOU WILL NEED
Don't be daunted

Your ravenous puppy needs to eat four times a day and grows on average 12 times faster than a human child, so choosing the right food for him is paramount. Canine diets can be just as complex and varied as human ones, containing varying levels of protein, carbohydrate (sugar), lipid (fat), vitamins and minerals from many different sources. With a multitude of diets available and making the

▲ It is important to give your fast-growing puppy the correct nutrition for his age.

right choice critical to your puppy's development, many owners find decisions regarding nutrition daunting. With information showered upon you by breeders, vets and other dog owners, the best piece of advice to remember is keep it simple. Whatever food you choose, always supply your puppy with fresh water.

COMMON QUESTIONS
feeding

How often and when do I feed my puppy?
Four times daily at evenly spaced intervals is recommended for an eight-week-old puppy, gradually reducing in frequency over time. Fresh water should be constantly available. Always feed your puppy after you have eaten – this is a good way to reinforce the message that he is subordinate to you and your family in the dominance hierarchy. Try to feed your puppy at around the same times every day and this will determine when he defecates (within 20 minutes or so after eating), resulting in easier housetraining.

Isn't it boring for a dog to feed him the same food all the time?
No. Dogs tend to eat and enjoy one type of food throughout their lives. If you offer them many different types of food, they will choose the one to eat based on taste, not on whether it is the best for them nutritionally. Also, changes in diet can cause gut upsets, leading to diarrhoea and weight loss. At the young puppy stage, you need to be firm in choosing a good-quality complete balanced food and sticking with it.

Dry versus moist diets

Dry complete foods are generally recommended over moist canned foods by vets, but there are advantages and disadvantages to both.

Dry diets are good for oral health, as they have an abrasive effect on the teeth when eaten. They are also relatively economical and, as they tend to be more concentrated with less volume than moist foods, produce a smaller amount of faeces.

Dry foods may, however, be less palatable to your dog than the moist varieties, as they have a less pronounced aroma. Moist foods also offer a wider choice. On the other hand, moist foods store poorly once opened and can readily attract flies in hot weather. A moist diet is also not beneficial to your dog's oral health.

Complete diets versus complementary foods and supplements

Complete diets are just that – complete. They do not require any additional supplements. In fact, giving your dog extra additives could be detrimental to his health. Complete diets make feeding straightforward, as all premium complete diets are nutritionally balanced. They also contain top-quality ingredients, resulting in a visibly healthy puppy. The downside is that these sorts of foods are relatively expensive.

Complementary foods (such as treats and chews) are those that have to be combined with other foods to provide for your puppy's nutritional needs. They are usually packaged in a semi-moist

▲ Dry complete foods are nutritionally balanced and can also be best in the long term for your puppy's dental health.

form. As they are not completely nutritionally balanced, complementary foods cannot form the sole basis of your dog's diet. Although adding dietary variety, they complicate feeding as you must combine carefully selected foodstuffs or supplements to give your puppy all that he requires.

Commercially prepared foods versus home-cooked meals

Commercial dog foods are mass-produced and specifically designed for optimal canine health. They are readily available and easy to use, but lack variability in texture.

Some breeders and owners still advocate and insist upon home-cooked meals. These have the advantage of containing fresh ingredients and offering variety. However, if you are cooking meals for your dog yourself, there is a risk that you won't provide all the necessary vitamins and minerals. Maintaining the optimum nutritional balance is not easy, especially if you have a growing puppy. A home-cooked diet is also time-consuming to prepare. If you opt for this method, ask your vet for advice and ensure that your puppy is regularly checked to detect any deficiencies before they irreparably damage his health.

▶ The exciting sights and sounds of a new home may distract your puppy from his food at first.

COMMON QUESTIONS
feeding

What happens if my puppy won't eat the food I offer him?

If a puppy doesn't eat the food as soon as you place it down, he probably won't eat it at all. Leave it for five minutes only, then pick it up, cover it and wait an hour or so. This wait will stimulate your puppy's appetite and avoids teaching him that if he won't eat one food, he will be immediately offered another. If he is really stubborn, try mixing his food with some warm water, which will increase its smell and soften it, helping to improve its palatability. Most puppies won't eat particularly well for the first few days in a new home, as there is so much excitement, exploration and playing to be done. Also, they may just not be hungry, so don't worry too much if they are not constantly devouring their food. Always consult a vet if you are concerned.

Is ordinary chocolate dangerous for dogs to eat?

Chocolate, or more accurately the active ingredient theobromine present in cocoa, is toxic to dogs. Eaten in large amounts, theobromine can cause bleeding disorders and severe diarrhoea in canines, which can prove fatal. In addition, grapes, onions and garlic should not be fed to dogs, since they are part of the deadly nightshade family and can be toxic if consumed in large quantities.

◄ Treats are very useful for training your puppy, but don't forget that they will affect his daily calorie count.

Treats

Treats and titbits will invariably be given to your puppy when training, but they must be taken into account when calculating the total amount of energy (calories) consumed each day by your puppy. Excess weight can cause extra stress on joints, lead to strain on the heart and liver and result in an unhealthy overweight adult dog.

Choose a treat that is meat-based or cereal-based and specifically designed for dogs. Human foods, such as sweet biscuits or potato crisps, offer little nutritional value to your puppy. It is suggested that over 40 per cent of the world's dogs are currently clinically obese. Strictly measuring out the food given to your puppy as meals or treats is an important start to keeping his weight under control in the long term.

Organic diets

There are also some dog foods available that are formulated with raw materials sourced only from high-quality organic farms. These sorts of organic foods should display a label of certification. Environmentally responsible products, they are as nutritionally balanced and as good quality as their non-organic counterparts, but unfortunately carry a higher price tag.

Vegetarian diets

Some dog owners are vegetarian and would like to feed their puppies with a similarly meat-free diet. This is not recommended. Solely vegetarian diets are nutritionally inadequate for puppies as canines are naturally carnivores (meat eaters). This kind of diet is very difficult to balance correctly and can easily cause nutrient deficiencies that could result in disease.

OLD WIVES' TAIL

Feeding a dog raw bones will make him become aggressive.

Raw bones will not make your dog aggressive. While cooked bones splinter and can cause constipation and obstruction, raw bones crush when bitten and are much safer for your dog to consume. However, all bones can potentially lodge in your puppy's gut so it is best to give chews specifically designed to improve your dog's dental health. Raw meat sourced from a respected butcher is acceptable, but animals can pick up parasites by consuming raw meat that is not of high hygienic quality. It can also be difficult to achieve a good balance of vitamins and minerals in home-prepared meals (see page 28), so keeping to complete balanced diets is easier and ultimately better for your dog than feeding him on raw meat.

Puppy- and breed-specific diets

You can buy specifically formulated puppy diets. Not just a marketing ploy, these are definitely worth considering because they contain higher nutrient levels to support the rapid rate of early growth in your puppy.

A breed-specific diet is another option that is well worth thinking about. Good-quality breed-specific diets take into account all your dog's requirements, as the manufacturers have studied the breed's particular development patterns to supply exactly the nutrients needed to promote optimal growth and health. These diets cater individually for large, medium and small breed dogs, aiming to meet the different and changing nutritional needs of each group as the dogs mature. Most offer a weight or age chart so that you can be sure to feed the right amounts of food as your puppy grows.

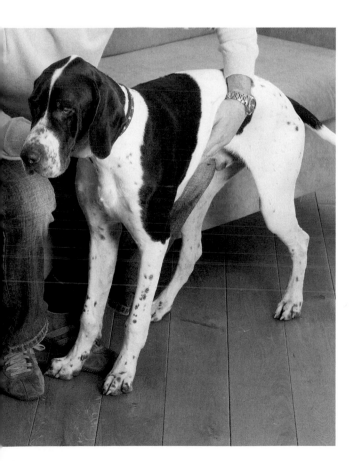

COMMON QUESTIONS
feeding

Can I change the food that the breeder was feeding my puppy?

Yes you can, as long as you do it gradually. There may be a few occasions in your puppy's life when you need to alter his diet, so slowly introduce the new food with the old so that the puppy gets used to the difference in size, flavour and/or texture. Sudden changes can result in diarrhoea, so change a diet gradually over a week and be prepared for some softer stools to be produced during that time.

How do I know if I am feeding my puppy the right food in the right amounts?

Regularly assess your puppy, checking that he has bright eyes, a glossy coat, wet nose and a bright disposition. A puppy should always have a visible 'waist' and ribs that can be felt, indicating that he is not becoming overweight. Arrange regular check-ups with your vet to confirm that you have your puppy on the right dietary track.

I have another dog. How will this affect feeding the puppy?

Feed your puppy after your adult dog has finished eating so that there is no possibility of annoyance or aggression from the older dog. Pick up any other dogs' or cats' bowls so that the puppy only has access to his own food.

◀ A puppy's ribs are a good indicator of his weight. If you can feel them easily, he is not overweight.

PUPPY PROOFING YOUR HOME AND GARDEN

Take pre-emptive action

Exploration and investigation of his environment and all that it contains are important and entertaining components of your new puppy's development. Since your adventurous puppy will be chewing, licking, pawing and nudging his way through your home, precautions need to be taken to avoid accident or injury to him, as well as to safeguard your property.

Think of your puppy's arrival in terms of a visiting human toddler with an amazing sense of smell and sharp teeth. You should assess what would prove inviting to such a child in your home and then move all these attractive, non-puppy items out of reach. By removing or eliminating potential hazards, you will ensure that your new puppy has a happy and relaxed arrival, minimize the risk of accidents and unnecessary vet bills and avoid the fallout of ruining your and your family's valued belongings.

Establish ground rules

Before your puppy arrives, it is best to lay down some basic ground rules with regard to where he can and can't go. Designate some rooms, such as bedrooms, out of bounds to your puppy to keep the cleaning up confined. Make sure that everyone in the family knows that these are puppy-free zones and use baby gates or closed doors to enforce the no-go areas. These rooms consequently won't need to be kept so tidy and the belongings within them will be safe from a chewing puppy.

Decide where your puppy will toilet – that is, which spot indoors or outdoors – and consider the installation of a dog flap if necessary. If he will be toileting outdoors, will he have the run of the garden or just a small section? Although puppies should be supervised at all times in the early days, you may suddenly and unavoidably need to be elsewhere, so defining where would be a safe room or 'den' for the puppy if you have to leave him alone briefly is also worth considering.

▲ Anything left on the floor will be fair game for your puppy, so keep items you don't want him to chew out of reach.

▶ Puppy proof your cupboards and avoid unwanted raids by rethinking where you keep foodstuffs.

Prepare puppy zones

Once you have decided which rooms he will be allowed to range freely in, go about puppy proofing them, considering both the safety of your puppy and the protection of your property. Keep all poisonous products and medicines out of the puppy's potential reach, tidy away dangling electrical wires and check for gaps that the puppy could get through or caught under.

The ways in which the most commonly used areas of the home – kitchen, living room and garden – should be puppy-proofed are described on pages 33–35.

Kitchen

Rubbish bin Choose a tall bin with a secure lid to avoid the puppy raiding it.

Floors Use non-toxic detergents for cleaning. As floors are generally slippery, avoid playing with your puppy on them. Keep your personal belongings off the floor to avoid them being chewed up or urinated on.

Cupboards Check for gaps beneath that the puppy could squeeze into and consider placing child safety locks on the doors to avoid him accessing the contents.

Appliances Your puppy may find it a great game to hide in open dishwashers, washing machines and refrigerators with potentially disastrous consequences, so make sure that they all close firmly. The oven should also be kept closed and you should get in the habit of turning saucepan handles inwards to prevent spillage.

Tea towels These are perfect for your puppy to chew on, so keep them out of his reach.

Food and drink Don't tempt a puppy to jump up by leaving food lying around. Unsupervised hot drinks can be spilled and lead to injury. Remember to tidy up straight away.

Living room

Televisions, lamps and other electrical equipment
Check for dangling cables and wires that may be fun for your puppy to tug on or chew.

Rugs During the early days, it is a good idea to roll up and store away any rugs that you value. They are prime candidates for chewing and your new puppy is also highly likely to urinate on them.

Coffee table If tables are quite low, don't leave food, drinks or papers on them as they are all items that your puppy will be keen to investigate.

Ornaments Any breakable objects need to be placed up high out of reach of the puppy or stored away to prevent accidents.

Belongings Shoes and slippers may have been left strewn around the living room before the puppy arrived, but this is no longer an option. If you want them kept intact, put them away.

Open fires A dangerous feature for puppies, who won't understand that they are a no-go zone. Puppy burns and sooty footprints await the owner who doesn't invest in a fireguard cover or partition.

Curtains and blinds Cords or blinds are great fun to play with, so tuck them away before your puppy discovers them.

▼ Coffee breaks are great for you, but not so great for puppy. Keep dangerous items off low coffee tables.

Garden

Boundary fences To keep your puppy safe and secure into adulthood, check for broken sections, holes and sharp edges. If you have hedges, look for gaps and fill them with meshing if necessary. The average fence height for containing a larger agile dog can exceed 2.5 metres (8 feet), while a small terrier would be adequately contained by a 1.2 metre (4 foot) fence. Ask your breeder what height is required to keep an adult dog contained.

Water Ponds, water features and swimming pools are all potentially deadly to the adventurous new arrival, so keep your puppy safe by fencing them off securely.

Plants and flower beds Whether they are prickly, poisonous or precious, plants are a constant source of amusement to a puppy. If you want to keep your plants intact and your puppy safe, fence them off or place pots up high until his chewing has diminished.

Garden shed Keep the door to a garden shed or other storage area securely locked, as it is likely to contain pesticides and other potentially hazardous substances and objects.

▲ Your puppy will investigate everywhere, finding trouble wherever it may be!

Gates Ensure that any gates to the outside world are secure. Replace locks if necessary and keep the gates safely closed at all times.

Hosepipe A perfect chewing toy, a hosepipe can be damaged by your puppy or he can get caught up in it. Keeping it wound up and out of reach can prevent mishaps.

To find out more on...
Chewing, go to page 124
Diarrhoea, go to page 140
Grooming, go to page 60
Puppy games, go to page 54
Settling in, go to page 45
Toilet training, go to page 46
Visiting the vet, go to page 37
Walking on a lead, go to page 69

The V.E.T.
Getting the best treatment

The veterinary clinic is an essential part of your new puppy's health care, but the mere sound of the word 'vet' can evoke a fearful response in many canine companions. Developing a good relationship with your vet early on will keep visits enjoyable, without resorting to spelling out the dreaded word V.E.T. to keep your puppy calm.

CHOOSING A GOOD VET

Do some market research

The service provided by veterinary clinics can vary dramatically. Visit the local practices without your puppy, checking services and approachability of staff. Focus on hygiene levels rather than on fees, as your puppy deserves the best treatment in a quality establishment. Ask other owners for advice, as most people are keen to speak highly of their vet if the service has been outstanding.

Count the cost

It is pertinent to reaffirm here that a dog is not cheap to own and all potential veterinary costs should be considered before you buy one. In the worst case scenario, your puppy may turn out to be a sickly or accident-prone individual and fees for veterinary treatment will be compounded by the cost of all the preventative medications and food essential for keeping him healthy.

WHEN TO GO AND WHAT TO EXPECT

Early introductions

To benefit both your puppy's health and behavioural development, it is a good idea to pay a visit to the vet in the first few days after the puppy's arrival. Introductions are a useful means of gauging your vet's approach, as he or she greets and examines your bundle of joy. Exposing the puppy to the clinic at this early stage is also a good way to develop a positive relationship with the establishment, in advance of more traumatizing visits for vaccinations and possibly surgical treatment.

Initial health check

Many puppies from reputable breeders come with a guarantee of health that gives you the right to return them if not in perfect condition, so it is paramount to have a vet check to confirm that the puppy is healthy before you develop a strong emotional bond. Many people become attached as soon as they set eyes on their chosen puppy, so it then becomes the vet's responsibility to do some straight talking and explain any possible problems when examining the puppy for the first time.

Vital first visit

Around eight weeks is the time for your young puppy's first visit to the vet. Vaccinations, worming and flea treatment may all be necessary at this age to ensure that your puppy remains healthy and develops normally. Fortnightly checks are recommended by many vets in the early stages to ensure healthy weight gain and avoid any potential health or behavioural problems developing.

Getting there

The journey to the vet alone can be enough to terrify your puppy. Keep him in a specially designed pet carry container lined with soft, absorbent and non-slip bedding and attach it to a fastened seat belt. If you have an open rear compartment in your vehicle, you can fit a wire cage for your puppy. Alternatively, a larger puppy can be fitted with a harness, which usually has a loop to attach to a seat belt to prevent him jumping around.

Plan your journey to keep the time that your puppy is travelling in the car to the barest minimum. Avoid frightening your puppy by closing doors quietly and driving carefully and smoothly around corners, over bumps and in traffic. Attract your puppy's attention by providing treats or toys. If your puppy seems very frightened or is sick when travelling in your car, see page 134 for advice.

▼ Consider investing in a puppy crate for trips to the vet, to transport your precious cargo safely.

MAKING VET VISITS FUN
Create positive associations
Many dogs have an innate fear of the V.E.T., which can make life difficult for you and the veterinary staff. The clinic's evocative sounds and smells only remind them of discomforts suffered on previous visits, so the fear is renewed whenever they come through the clinic doors. To avoid negative associations, give treats and toys before, during and after any visit to the vet to keep the experience as positive as possible. Ask your vet to give your puppy a treat after the examination, and ensure that lots of love is bestowed on him in reward for good behaviour. Avoid responding immediately to nervous behaviour, since this may reinforce irrational fears.

▼ A puppy party at the vet's is a safe and enjoyable means of introducing your pet to other canines.

Socialize with the staff
Take the opportunity to socialize your new charge thoroughly by allowing veterinary nurses and support staff to approach and interact with him. It is, however, recommended that your puppy avoids contact with other dogs until after the second booster vaccination is given (see page 66), unless you are absolutely sure that the other dogs have been fully vaccinated. To avoid your puppy developing a fear of the vet, visit the clinic regularly for weight checks, when your puppy can enjoy the experience without being on the receiving end of a sharp needle.

Attend a puppy party
Many veterinary clinics host puppy parties, which consist of a group of up to seven young puppies invited to the clinic for an evening of fun and

▶ The full course of vaccinations against disease will be completed around 10–12 weeks.

education. The party runs for one to two hours and is generally free. Puppies usually attend between 9 and 12 weeks of age. It is an excellent way to socialize your young puppy by meeting other similar-sized and aged dogs along with owners and veterinary staff, in a relaxed, safe and monitored environment. A puppy party provides your dog with a positive and happy experience of a visit to the clinic. It also offers you the ideal way to be informally introduced to your veterinary practice, the staff and the services they provide, and to learn valuable behavioural and health-care tips.

PREVENTATIVE HEALTH CARE
Providing protection
Various measures can be taken to ensure that your puppy is kept safe from potential diseases and parasites that can cause ill health. A young puppy is at the mercy of many harmful infections and pests lurking in his everyday environment against which he has little defence. The use of preventative medications helps to bolster your puppy's immune system and protect him while he grows into a healthy adult dog.

Vaccinations
These are injections given to your puppy to stimulate his immune system to fight disease. There are many life-threatening viral diseases that infect dogs (such as those listed on page 41) and vaccinations help to produce antibodies to protect your puppy against them. Your puppy is given some protection from these diseases through his mother's milk in the first few hours of life. Colostrum is produced by the mammary glands of the bitch immediately after giving birth to puppies. Rich in maternal antibodies, colostrum provides essential protection for a puppy up to around 12 weeks of age. Vaccinations are started at six to eight weeks of age, then repeated at around 10 to 12 weeks, to ensure that your puppy is protected before maternal antibody levels wane.

OLD WIVES' TAIL
I have had dogs for over 20 years and have never had them inoculated, so I don't believe in vaccinations in dogs.

This is an ill-considered conclusion, as the fact that no serious illnesses have resulted is a case of pure good luck. The diseases preventable by vaccination are still prevalent today and outbreaks are more likely to occur as concentrations of dogs in built-up areas continue to increase.

◀ At eight weeks a puppy needs to visit the vet for his first set of vaccinations.

Worming

Intestinal or gut worms are a common parasite in puppies, causing vomiting, diarrhoea, reduced growth and anaemia. An indication of infestation is a puppy licking excessively around his rear end, a pot-bellied appearance or an inability to put on weight. There are at least 12 different species of gut worms known to parasitize the intestinal tract of a puppy, with infections occurring from birth via suckling mum's milk and the puppy's environment. Some of these parasites are transmissible to humans, so keeping your puppy free of worms also helps to protect your family's health.

Medication to treat worms comes in liquid, paste, tablet or topical liquid form, depending on the weight of your dog and the specific worms to be treated. Flexibility is needed when choosing wormers, as some forms can cause stomach upsets in certain puppies. The most effective treatments for all four types of gut worm are available from your vet; some preparations are flavoured to ensure ease of administration.

The breeder, pet shop owner or welfare worker should have given at least one worming treatment to your puppy prior to you taking him home. Worming should be continued fortnightly for the first three months of life, monthly until six months, then every three months as an adult dog.

The different types of worm treated include roundworm, tapeworm, hookworm and whipworm:

Roundworm The most common worm in puppies, this parasite has a similar appearance to a small earthworm, although pale in colour. It causes a pot-bellied appearance in its host and the puppy can seem generally weak with a dull coat and reduced growth.

Tapeworm This larger, segmented parasitic worm will appear as 'grains of rice' in your puppy's faeces. Attaching itself to the intestine, the worm sheds eggs contained within segments of its body into the faeces and can cause diarrhoea and vomiting in a heavily infected puppy.

Vaccinations are mostly given in the form of an injection under the skin of the neck, called the 'scruff'. Be prepared for your puppy to make a little whimper when the needle goes in, with some puppies experiencing slight discomfort or itching over the site for a few minutes afterwards. Many puppies will feel a little low after their first vaccination – tiredness and poor appetite are common signs over the following 12 hours. If these symptoms persist longer than 12 hours or are more severe, contact your vet.

With the positive effects of vaccination greatly outweighing any potential side effects, annual booster vaccinations are recommended for dogs throughout their lives to maintain strong immunity to these potentially fatal diseases. Most vets will send out reminders of your puppy's future vaccinations, but in any case forward-date your calendar to ensure that this important health precaution is not forgotten.

Common diseases prevented through vaccination

Parvovirus	A nasty viral disease causing severe vomiting and bloody diarrhoea, leading to rapid collapse and death, sometimes within 24 hours. Few puppies survive an infection of parvovirus.
Canine distemper	This highly infectious and contagious disease is often fatal and causes permanent disability and deformity in survivors. With the advent of routine vaccinations, this disease is now rarely reported.
Infectious canine hepatitis	Attacking the liver, this virus can cause sudden death in puppies within 24 to 36 hours. Survivors often suffer with long-term liver disease or become carriers, spreading the disease to other canines.
Leptospirosis	Two forms of this bacterium exist, which are spread by the urine of carrier animals, notably the rat. One form causes acute illness and jaundice; the other, a slower insidious form, results in chronic deterioration of the liver and kidneys.
Canine parainfluenza	Commonly known as the virus causing 'kennel cough', parainfluenza infection leads to a harsh, dry cough that can take up to 10 days to resolve.
Bordetella bronchiseptica	A bacterial infection associated with canine parainfluenza, the flu-like symptoms can dramatically worsen, resulting in a thick, purulent nasal discharge and chest infection. It is vaccinated against with a nasal spray and this specific inoculation is used mainly when animals are known to be visiting high exposure risk areas, such as boarding kennels.
Rabies	Endemic to the USA and Southern European nations, this virus is being increasingly vaccinated against as pet travel becomes more widespread. All pet passports require a vaccination against rabies, to prevent transmission of the disease and avoid the need for pet quarantine. A blood test is generally needed to prove an adequate immunity to rabies, the sample being taken at least 30 days after the initial rabies vaccination.

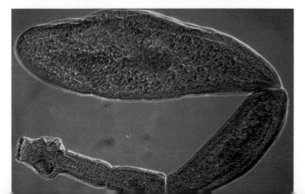

◀ Roundworm (top) and tapeworm (bottom) are the most common worms in puppies.

Hookworm Much less common than the above two parasites, this worm is a blood sucker that attaches itself to the intestinal wall, causing bleeding and anaemia.

Whipworm This least common worm is mainly caught via exposure to the faeces of an infected dog through digging or when taking your puppy to the park. Once finding its way into your puppy's intestines, it attaches to the gut wall, causing bloody diarrhoea and weight loss.

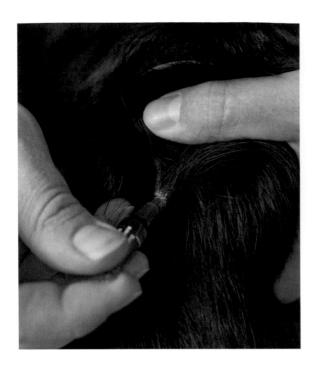

◀ A topical treatment supplied by your vet is the best way of dealing with fleas.

traditional medications within flea populations. Topical treatments from your vet, such as spot-ons or certain sprays, tend to be most effective; unfortunately shampoos, collars, sprays and powders seem to have only a short-term or limited effect on these irritating insects. Check the label to ensure that the treatment is safe for the age of your puppy, and always use as instructed. If a flea infestation is detected, it is worthwhile treating your home with topical sprays to avoid dormant eggs hatching at a later date.

Tick, lice and mite control
Ticks, lice and mites are also common external parasites in puppies and can vary greatly in prevalence according to region, climate and breed.

▼ Fleas (top) and ticks (bottom) are both external parasites found on dogs. Consult your vet for advice on treatment.

Flea control
Visible to the naked eye, fleas are the most common external parasite affecting canines, causing both puppies and owners to itch just at the thought of them! The bites of these blood-sucking parasites tend to cause a mild allergic reaction, making your puppy itch and leading to skin damage and infection. Fleas also play a role in the transmission of tapeworm between animals and in addition can cause severe anaemia (see page 140) in very young puppies because they can consume up to 15 times their own body weight in blood per day.

Living in the coats of dogs (and cats), fleas can also set up residence in the carpets of heated homes, resulting in bites shared with human inhabitants. With up to 50 eggs produced daily by a well-fed mature female flea during her 100-day plus lifespan, infestation of your home can rapidly occur unless regular preventative treatments are used. The presence of fleas can be easily detected by looking for specks of black flea dirt within your puppy's coat, or for signs of itching or skin disease.

Treatments are constantly changing to keep up with the rapid development of resistance to

Ticks Exceedingly hardy, blood-sucking creatures, ticks are known disease carriers in certain parts of the world.

Lice These parasites tend to resemble flaking skin that accumulates behind the ears, causing a puppy to scratch around the head.

Mites Harvest mites appear as orange grains in the fur and can be extremely irritating. This category also includea demodex and the mites that cause sarcoptic mange, which burrow into the skin causing severe skin infection and disease.

Treatments for ticks, lice and mites can be used in a preventative or post-infection manner – certain flea medications are known to have an effect on some of these parasites, preventing infections from occurring. Always consult your vet if you suspect a parasitic infection, to ensure that the correct treatment is implemented promptly.

MICROCHIPPING YOUR PUPPY

How it works

Used to identify permanently a myriad of creatures ranging from horses to tortoises, microchipping is highly recommended for a newly purchased or re-homed puppy. A microchip is a small device the size of a grain of rice that is placed under the dog's skin. It contains a number that can be detected by a scanner passed over the area where it has been placed. This number is held with your contact details in the microchip company's database and allows a lost animal to be returned to its rightful owner from any welfare clinic, vet clinic or government organization possessing an appropriate scanner.

How and when to do it

The vet uses a large needle to place the microchip under the skin over the neck or 'scruff'. As the placement of the microchip can cause a little discomfort to your puppy, it can either be done at the initial vaccination stage or when the booster vaccination is given (see page 66). Alternatively, microchipping can be carried out at the same time as a neutering procedure under anaesthetic (see page 110).

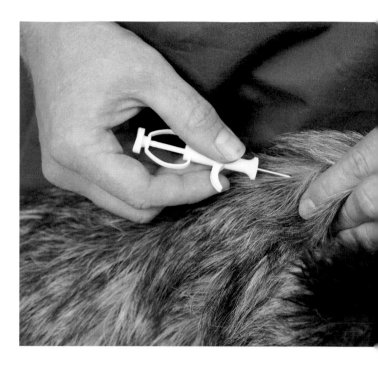

▲ A microchip placed under the skin at the neck will enable a lost puppy to be identified and returned home.

To find out more on...

Alternative medicines and therapies,
    go to page 152
Anaemia, go to page 140
Common puppy illnesses, go to page 138
Kennel cough, go to page 139
Neutering, go to page 110
Nursing your sick puppy, go to page 142
Puppy first aid, go to page 143
Resuscitation, go to page 146
Travel sickness and car phobia,
    go to page 134

Bringing your puppy home

The first few days

Moving to a new environment can be very upsetting for your puppy, but there is much you can do to ease the transition. From day one you should also be starting the processes of toilet training and socialization, as well as learning how your canine communicates. But there will be plenty of scope for fun and games too!

TRAVELLING HOME
Provide comfort and security

It is best to collect your new puppy in the evening when he will probably have already been fed and will be naturally drowsy. He should then be settled and with luck will fall asleep on the journey home. Bring blankets with you to wrap your puppy in, rubbing them on mum and his littermates before you leave – these smells will comfort your puppy during the drive to his new home and during the coming days.

It is a good idea to transport your puppy in a cardboard box or a pet carry container, lined with a puppy training pad or absorbent paper and the scented towel. The box or carry container should be secured by a seat belt for maximum safety, or a passenger can keep firm hold of it. The driver should drive smoothly, taking special care not to disturb the puppy.

SETTLING IN
Take it gently

On arrival home, keep excitement to a minimum, playing with the puppy for only a short while and allowing him briefly to explore his new home. Offer a small meal of whatever food he was fed previously, then give him the opportunity to use either a puppy training pad or the garden to toilet before introducing him to where he will sleep and putting him to bed.

Surviving the first night

There are different schools of thought regarding a puppy's first night at home and how it should be handled. Some people believe that puppies should be acclimatized to the sleeping arrangements in a house gradually, while others think you should start as you mean to continue by keeping your puppy in another room and ignoring the crying and whining that is likely to take place at first. Both of these approaches have their merits.

Keeping the puppy near you makes sense, as dogs are naturally pack animals and survive on the comfort and security of others. But sooner or later you will need to begin leaving your puppy alone, so

getting him used to sleeping on his own from the beginning is a good idea. If you feel that you really can't leave him alone for the first night, then you should sleep with the puppy in the room in which you wish him to continue sleeping. Allowing him to sleep in your bedroom – or even worse, your bed – can result in a puppy that cannot bear being without you or lead to separation disorders developing later in life.

BETTY'S DIARY
coming home

Day 1 After bidding her loving breeder goodbye, my beautiful eight-week-old Border Terrier puppy and I began our hour-long journey home. She proved to be a good traveller, settling well into her carry container, which was constantly opened during the drive to gaze upon my precious cargo.

On arriving home, Betty waddled around the living room, ate well and played – showing early signs of her brilliance by understanding the concept of fetch on her very first day! When put into her crate for bedtime, I prepared myself for whining, as she nestled into her mum-scented blanket in the en-suite bathroom adjoining my room. It was understandable that Betty should be upset at being confined on her own in a strange new place after enjoying the company of mum and three siblings until now. Her whining, though, was worse than I had imagined, and continued for some long hours until I finally cajoled her to sleep with soothing words. Little did I know that the worst was yet to come . . .

Lessons learned

Be prepared for a bad first night and try to ensure that you don't have to go to work the next day, just in case of sleep deprivation!

Easing his distress

The generally recommended approach is to place the puppy in a crate lined with bedding and a puppy training pad (see page 47). A heated pad or hot-water bottle tucked into the bedding is also a good idea, to mimic the heat generated by other sleeping puppies and mum. This will help your puppy to feel secure in another room from where you sleep, and you will be comforted to know that he is contained and safe. A dog-appeasing pheromone product or DAP (see page 133), either sprayed directly onto bedding or in the form of a diffuser, will be very helpful in settling your puppy into his new home.

SLEEPING ALONE

Help him to acclimatize

For the first few nights, it is almost certain that your puppy will be restless, whine and whimper. Don't be tempted to go into him when he cries, as this will reinforce the expectation that he will gain your attention if he vocalizes. Making this early mistake will result in a more insistent puppy and lengthen the time taken for him to cope with sleeping alone. Playing background music or talking to him from

▲ A puppy crate provides the perfect refuge for your new arrival – a place all of his own to which he can retreat.

another room can help comfort him without you needing to get up when called.

Expect an average of around six hours of sleep a night for the first few weeks. This period will extend in length as the puppy becomes acclimatized to sleeping alone and you both settle into a routine.

TOILET TRAINING

Your greatest challenge

The single biggest cause of owner despair during the early days of dog ownership is attempting, and failing, to housetrain the new arrival. Toilet training is a process that requires an abundance of patience on your part. Instinctively, puppies will urinate away from where they sleep, actively performing this behaviour in the wild from around three weeks of age. Dogs in the home environment behave in the same manner, so training is needed to teach your puppy that inside your home is a non-toileting zone and that outdoors is where they should be going.

First steps

Initially use a puppy training pad, placed in the corner of a room. Training pads are impregnated with a hormone that, when smelt by your puppy, will stimulate him to urinate on the pad. When you are unable to monitor his activities indoors, place the puppy in his crate or play pen to limit where he goes. Line the crate or pen with plastic sheeting and absorbent material for easy cleaning.

It is recommended that as soon as possible you should begin taking him outside to toilet, so that you don't have to train him twice – once to go indoors on a mat, then again to go outside. Lots of love, attention and even food treats should be given when the puppy toilets in the correct spot, to reinforce the lesson learned.

Planned toileting

Establish a routine of feeding and walking so that you can begin to judge when your puppy is most likely to toilet. Most puppies will defecate within 20 minutes of eating, so you can maximize your success rate by planning to walk your puppy outside around that time. Remembering to take this precaution will help to avoid any accidents, keeping your home clean and, above all, stress free. Most puppies tend to be fully housetrained by around six months of age, although you should be prepared to accept that occasional mistakes can be made up until one year of age.

▼ Absorbent training pads can be used at first, to give your puppy something to aim for indoors.

RECIPES FOR TOILET TRAINING SUCCESS

Be proactive

Actively take your puppy into the garden or outside area every hour, after eating and drinking, after exercise and immediately on waking and before going to bed. In this way, you can seize the opportunity when he needs to go, giving him the best chance to do it in the right spot.

Establish a standard command

Use a command such as 'go wee' when he is going to the toilet. In time, this command will become synonymous with the action of going to the toilet and he will begin going on demand.

Reinforce with rewards

Reward your puppy when he goes in the right place, lavishing treats and praise on him, to reinforce positively the lesson that going outside is correct. The puppy gains from performing correctly and begins associating toileting outside with happy, positive feelings.

Take corrective action

Only reprimand your puppy when you actually see him go in an inappropriate spot, calling out a loud 'no' to interrupt him. Then quickly call him to follow you to the door, walking him out to the correct position to complete his toileting. If you can interrupt him long enough to get him to follow you outside, he will begin to learn the two parts of going to the toilet correctly: first, asking to go out by walking to the door; and second, actually going to the toilet outside.

Avoid post-accident reprimands

Don't reprimand your puppy if you find any 'presents' indoors. Telling a puppy off after the event will only frighten him and possibly cause a setback in all other areas of his behavioural development because he will have no idea what you are shouting about.

It's a good idea to clean up the mess out of your puppy's sight, as your body language will scream your displeasure and annoyance, which your puppy will be able to detect. Consequently, he will go in more obscure places next time to avoid your wrath. These places will be harder to locate and you will be less likely to catch him in the act. Use a biological cleaner to ensure that you remove his scent. Less powerful cleaners may allow the scent to remain, stimulating him to toilet in that same spot again.

▼ Actively walking your new puppy in the garden every hour will dramatically increase the chances of toilet training success.

Learn to read the warning signs

Walking in circles while sniffing the floor is a sure indication that your puppy needs to go to the toilet. Learning to recognize this basic canine behaviour gives you the chance to intervene before he toilets inside, walking him outside to wherever you would like him to go.

CONVERSING IN CANINE

Vocalizations

Complementing body posturing (see page 50), the use of vocalizations is an important means by which a dog expresses himself. Barking, growling, yowling, howling, whining, whimpering, squeaking and screaming all indicate different emotional states, depending upon the pitch of their delivery, and tend to be fairly self-explanatory. Low-pitched sounds are more menacing, threatening or a warning to stay away; conversely, a higher-pitched noise invites the opposite response.

▲ If your puppy starts sniffing the floor, it's a message to you that he needs to go!

COMMON QUESTIONS
toilet training

How do I toilet train my puppy when I don't have a garden?

Housetraining a puppy living in a flat may be more difficult and take a little more time, especially as the first few weeks of life must be spent in the safety of your home. Using a puppy training pad in a low-traffic part of your apartment will teach the basics of toilet training until your puppy has had all his vaccinations and can go out. Walking him regularly is then the key to success, finding a small patch of grass near your home for quick access. Bring a section of soiled puppy training pad with you, as smelling his urine scent may stimulate him to go outdoors. Make sure that you thoroughly reward him with attention and praise when he toilets where you intended him to go.

In these circumstances it is likely that he will continue to go indoors for longer than a puppy with access to an outside area from the outset, but with extra patience and dedication he will eventually achieve housetrained status.

I have been trying to housetrain my puppy for some while now, and he just doesn't seem to be improving. What should I do?

In this situation, it is best to consult your vet or a local behaviourist (see page 117). Urinary infections and disorders are uncommon at this early age, but can be the underlying reason why a puppy is struggling with housetraining. Alternatively, inherent behavioural problems, such as fearfulness or unconscious mistakes made by you in training, could be causing his slow progress. These issues can be quickly resolved with the help of an animal behaviourist, to avoid toileting indoors becoming a learned and normal behaviour for your puppy.

READING HIS BODY LANGUAGE

What is your puppy telling you?

Although dogs don't understand human languages, they can interpret verbal commands, especially when used in conjunction with a physical gesture. In the same way that our facial gestures complement our spoken words, a dog similarly uses body posture to reflect his feelings. A greater understanding of your puppy will come from a knowledge of his basic body language, which is used in canine interactions to diffuse physical aggression and foster friendly encounters. It is also important to understand vocalizations, which indicate when your puppy may be frightened, frustrated or feeling in a playful mood (see page 51). Learning to understand the differences between your puppy's senses and your own (see page 52) is also invaluable in helping you to tailor training and games to your new canine companion and to develop the bond between you.

Tail Originally designed to assist with balance, the tail is the part of a dog's body language best understood by humans. A wagging tail is a common sign of a contented and happy dog and the faster it wags, the happier and more confident or enthusiastic a dog is in that particular situation. The tail position is also a strong indicator of a dog's emotional state: a tail held high is a sign of a dominant, stimulated or confident dog, while a tail between the legs indicates nervousness, fear or submission.

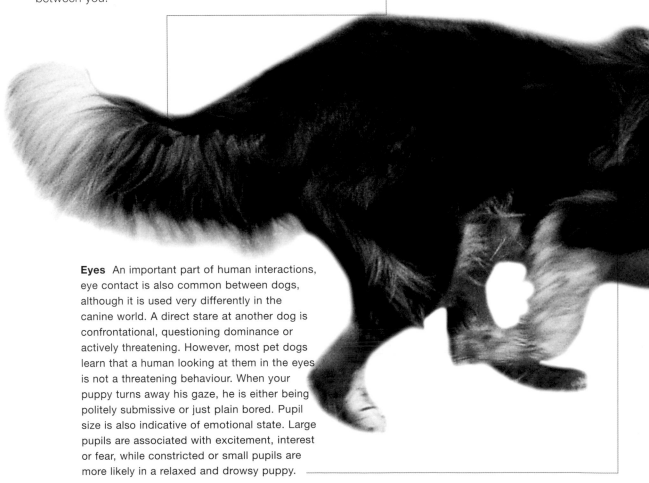

Eyes An important part of human interactions, eye contact is also common between dogs, although it is used very differently in the canine world. A direct stare at another dog is confrontational, questioning dominance or actively threatening. However, most pet dogs learn that a human looking at them in the eyes is not a threatening behaviour. When your puppy turns away his gaze, he is either being politely submissive or just plain bored. Pupil size is also indicative of emotional state. Large pupils are associated with excitement, interest or fear, while constricted or small pupils are more likely in a relaxed and drowsy puppy.

Ears Although very different in shape depending on the breed, dog's ears are able to transmit a wide range of emotions. Your puppy's ear placement will give much insight into how he is feeling, for example ears held back or flat against his head signify fear, aggression or submission. Erect or forward-placed ears indicate that your puppy is feeling confident, alert and ready for action.

Eyebrows The shape and position of the eyebrows can fluctuate. Relatively more eye exposed and creased eyebrows reveals your puppy's anger; relatively less eye exposed and relaxed brows signals a passive emotional state.

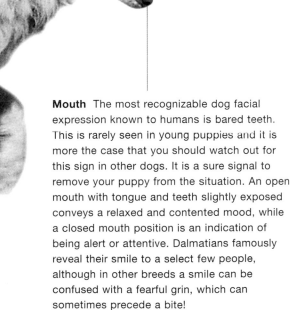

Mouth The most recognizable dog facial expression known to humans is bared teeth. This is rarely seen in young puppies and it is more the case that you should watch out for this sign in other dogs. It is a sure signal to remove your puppy from the situation. An open mouth with tongue and teeth slightly exposed conveys a relaxed and contented mood, while a closed mouth position is an indication of being alert or attentive. Dalmatians famously reveal their smile to a select few people, although in other breeds a smile can be confused with a fearful grin, which can sometimes precede a bite!

YOUR PUPPY'S STANCE
Showing how he feels

A puppy's posture varies dramatically, with different types of stance expressing different emotions. The play bow is a common body stance for a puppy, with bent front legs, a stretched back and tail in the air, and a sure indication that he is in the mood for a game. A stiff-legged, upright posture, with the fur standing up on his neck, can indicate fear, dominance or aggression. If he lies down with his legs stretched out to the side, he is feeling secure enough to rest in this vulnerable position. Rolling on his back with hind legs raised and head back is the ultimate form of submission, and an open invitation to rub his tummy.

▼ A play bow (top) is a sign of a friendly, playful puppy. When he rolls on his back (bottom), he is assuming a submissive or trusting posture.

PUPPY SENSES

Sight

Surprisingly poor in comparison to humans, dogs are thought to see the world in shades of yellow, green and grey. Darker colours, such as blue, appear more like black to a dog, while lighter colours are seen in hues of grey. Consequently, using blue, red or white toys works best, as they contrast well with green grass.

Smell

Scientists have estimated that a dog's sense of smell is between 10,000 and 1 million times as sensitive as ours and your puppy's sense of smell will never cease to astound you. Dogs have helped their owners for centuries in the search for food by using their highly attuned noses.

Hearing

The biggest difference between your hearing and your puppy's is at the high-frequency range. High-pitched sounds are used in dog whistles to gain dogs' attention at long distances. At levels undetectable to the human ear, high-pitched sounds emanating from the television set or vacuum cleaner can explain why some puppies bark at them. Generally, a dog's sense of hearing is thought to be around ten times as sensitive as ours, which is why many become nervous around loud noises such as fireworks.

Taste

With a sense of taste far less sensitive than ours, dogs are known for having a sweet tooth. They do not share our craving for salty foods, due to a chiefly meat-based diet naturally high in salts. Your puppy must be closely monitored in the home to avoid access to sweet substances that can be dangerous. Attraction to such sweet-tasting household items such as chocolate or vehicle anti-freeze is common in dogs and consumption of these can prove fatal (see page 150).

Touch

Dogs use touch in a similar way to humans, to gauge temperature, exert pressure on the body or on things in their environment and to perceive pain. One of the most important reasons why dogs are such perfect companions for humans is their use of touch to communicate. Strongly associated with emotion, the use of touch is paramount in communicating with your puppy and developing a close bond with him.

HOW YOUR PUPPY LEARNS

Lessons from nature

As a pack animal, a puppy's early lessons are learned through play and mimicking other animals in his group. At eight weeks of age, your puppy has already learned vital lessons from his mother and siblings and is now ready to be moulded into the dog you would like him to be around people.

Hierarchy in the wild pack is crucial to individual wellbeing. Each member knows his own place and works with the others as a team, without aggression, in order to maximize the pack's chances of survival. Understanding the importance of exerting dominance over your puppy without the need for physical punishment is supremely important to ensure a calm household and a contented dog.

Wild dogs rarely vocalize, using body language to converse with each other. For humans, however, verbal communication is much more important, so

◄ A dog whistle uses high-frequency sounds to call your puppy to you.

the use of verbal commands with obvious physical gestures is the best approach in teaching your puppy what you would like him to do.

Rewards for good behaviour

Attention and affection must be earned and considered as much of a treat as a dog chew. If it helps, think of your puppy as a demanding child – giving him attention for bad behaviour will only encourage him to act in the same way again. Only reward good manners and calm behaviour, ignoring bad behaviour and mistakes. Use food rewards where necessary to enable your puppy to understand when he has behaved correctly.

Trial and error

Trial and error is a common learning process in canine behaviour, as it is in human behaviour. In this way, your puppy can begin to appreciate the relationship between a behaviour and its consequence, either positive or negative. Learning from mistakes and gaining positively from success are powerful tools that you can use to train your puppy. For example, a puppy that is only given attention when quiet will quickly realize that barking leads to an affection deficiency.

PLAYING WITH YOUR PUPPY

Establish mutual trust

Play is a crucial element in your new puppy's development and an excellent way for you to form a strong friendship with him. Playing regularly with your puppy will enhance his willingness to please when it comes to basic training. It also reinforces in his mind the concept that people are sources of fun and entertainment, leading to a more sociable, happy and well-balanced adult dog.

Play helps to overcome your puppy's fear of the unknown, encouraging his confidence by diverting his attention away from aspects of his environment that may have previously worried him. Exercising his intellect and natural instincts, game playing stimulates his senses and burns off some of that excess puppy energy until he can safely venture into the great outdoors.

▲ Reinforce good behaviour with food rewards, praise or a game with a favourite toy.

Remain top dog

Wild dog puppies will play fight with each other in a battle of will and strength to assert their position in the hierarchy. Bearing this in mind, any game instituted with your puppy must result in you winning the majority of the time and keeping hold of the toy in question. This teaches the puppy very early on who is boss, setting boundaries of behaviour that he will need to adhere to in order to stay in favour with you.

Outlaw rough play

An important aspect to remember is that you are playing human–dog games, not dog–dog games, which involve the use of teeth. Any rough play, such as directly pushing your puppy, scuffling on the floor or encouraging biting or grabbing of hands or clothes (whether intentional or otherwise) should be banned. These types of activities can stimulate your puppy to bite. However soft and harmless at this early stage, rough play starts a pattern of behaviour that can become dangerous at a later stage. If your puppy's teeth come in contact with your skin during any activity, even accidentally, immediately cease the game to teach him that biting means no more play.

PUPPY GAMES

Tug of war

This well-known game is enjoyed by many puppies, but is one that must be carefully considered. Always win more encounters than you lose, otherwise your puppy will believe himself to be stronger than you and challenge your authority. Once you have won, the toy used in the game must be kept from the puppy and put out of reach, otherwise he will believe that he has won the encounter and kept the prize.

Never pull too hard or lift the puppy from the ground with the toy, as this can damage his teeth or mouth. If you regard your puppy as overly dominant in temperament, this may be a game to avoid altogether.

Treasure hunt

This game uses your puppy's superior sense of smell to hunt down food treats placed around the home for him to find. It is an entertaining game that all puppies will love, but hound dogs elevate it into an art form. Searching for food is a natural instinct in all dogs and this game encourages your puppy to put aside any fears he may have and explore his environment in pursuit of a tasty treat.

▶ Sniffing out treat-laden toys around the house is a fun game, especially for hound breed puppies.

▲ Terriers love a game of tug of war as it brings their shake and kill instincts to the fore.

Start by placing the treats while your puppy watches you, giving him a command such as 'find' or 'seek' before letting him loose. Once he has mastered this, make the game more difficult by hiding treats and toys around the home or garden without him watching. Some toys can be bought impregnated with a scent, while others, such as kongs, can be covered with a liver spray available from pet stores or filled with edible treats. This

▶ Other pets in your house need to be introduced to your puppy early on to avoid potential fear or aggression.

simple yet rewarding game encourages the intrepid explorer that is inherent in all puppies and will dramatically increase his confidence in, and enjoyment of, your home.

Fetch

A favourite since dogs were first domesticated, a game of fetch can be enjoyed with your puppy from his arrival at your home. Although fetching is an inherent ability found in gundogs such as retrievers, all breeds can be taught to fetch and this will bring added interest to walks in the future.

Start by tossing a rubber toy to gain his attention. When the puppy picks up the toy, call him back and give him a treat when he returns it to you. In order to pick up the treat, he will need to drop the ball, so use the verbal command 'drop' when he performs the required action. Food treats can soon be phased out, as playing the game becomes reward enough in itself, with all the fuss and attention that the puppy receives when he returns with the tossed item. Avoid using the traditional stick for this game, as it can splinter or be swallowed. It is safest to use tennis balls or rubber toys.

SOCIALIZATION AND HABITUATION
Build confidence

Both socialization and habituation are important processes identified by animal behaviourists as means of helping a puppy venture forth confidently into a domestic environment.

Socialization

A socialization programme will teach your puppy how to recognize and interact with his own species and all the other species that he will come across in everyday life. Socialization with humans and other dogs is vital for your puppy's development, teaching him social skills, dispelling his fears and encouraging a relaxed and well-balanced temperament in all environments.

In order to help socialize your puppy, begin to introduce him as soon as possible to the different people and animals listed below. (Bear in mind the restrictions on mixing with dogs of unknown vaccination status prior to your puppy completing his full course of vaccinations at 10 to 12 weeks.)

☐ **A variety of people of different ages and sex:** men, women, young children in prams and pushchairs, older children, elderly people
☐ **People in different outfits:** wearing hats, glasses, costumes, uniforms, helmets, masks
☐ **People moving or travelling in different ways:** running, walking, on scooters, bikes, rollerblades and skateboards
☐ **A variety of animals:** other dogs, cats, horses, livestock, small mammals such as guinea pigs, rabbits and other pets such as tortoises (always keep a firm hold of your puppy, to avoid a dangerous situation developing)

Habituation

Habituation is the process of accustoming your puppy to non-threatening objects, environments and experiences so that he learns to ignore rather than fear them. Exposing your puppy to a variety of objects and places in a calm, patient way will encourage exploration and help prevent irrational fears developing.

Start with everything found in your home until he can go out for walks when his vaccinations are completed, then begin exposing him to all the potentially frightening things that inhabit the great outdoors. It is vital for the new puppy parent to avoid comforting the puppy when he displays irrational fear of objects that he has been exposed to. Allow him time to calm down and begin investigation, responding with encouragement, praise and affection when he does so.

Help to habituate your puppy fully by exposing him to the items on the following checklist:

☐ **Novel environments:** friends' houses, vet clinics, bus stops, railway stations, shopping malls, parks, playgrounds
☐ **Novel objects:** cars, bicycles, household appliances such as the vacuum cleaner, mobile phones, children's toys, new puppy toys
☐ **Novel sounds:** thunderstorms, children's screams/cries/play, fireworks, traffic, aeroplanes, trains
☐ **Novel experiences:** being groomed, being examined by you and the vet, being picked up, being rolled over, going for walks, going on public transport, travelling in cars, in lifts and on escalators, being left alone for short periods of time

MEETING CATS

Control their contact

If you already have a cat and decide on a feline–canine union, ensure that you have the means to separate the animals from each other. A baby gate, play pen or crate works well to segregate an over-exuberant puppy, with a scratching post or basket kept out of reach for the retreating feline. If they have to be left alone together, always keep your puppy in a secured area so that the cat can choose to interact with him or keep well away. Introduce your puppy to your cat at an early age and chaperone any interaction so that you can moderate behaviour on both sides before the puppy gets over-excited or the cat becomes fearful or aggressive.

Manage meetings

Keep meetings brief and always allow your cat a chance to escape, reserving a room or two of the home as a puppy-free zone. Restrain your puppy but not your cat so that the latter can choose his proximity to the new arrival and your puppy cannot

◀ Expose your puppy to lots of different environments and he will soon feel at home wherever he goes.

▲ Avoid territorial aggression by introducing your puppy to other canines in a neutral place such as a friend's home.

give chase. Reward both cat and puppy for good behaviour when interacting with one another.

Problems can occur when you have a confident puppy that likes to bounce and lunge at the cat, since he knows it will then run and provide him with something to chase. If this happens, distract your puppy with toys and treats so that you are always the focus of games and fun, not the unimpressed feline.

Be patient and understanding

In most cases, puppies will quickly learn respect for housemate cats – the superiority complex of a feline is useful in teaching a puppy good manners. When raised with cats, most dog breeds will learn to accept them. Slowly, your cat will become used

to the puppy smell and, as long as a concerted effort is made by all family members to give your feline the same affection as is lavished on your puppy, your household should eventually become a calm and happy one.

MEETING OTHER DOGS
Find some neutral ground

If you decide on a new puppy in addition to an existing dog, the first meeting is best staged on virgin territory for both dogs and in an environment guaranteed disease free. A good site might be a friend's house or garden with no other dogs or an area of your own home where your resident dog has not previously ventured, such as a bathroom or bedroom. Choosing neutral ground will mean that your current dog will not feel the need to exert territorial dominance or aggression, and will be interested in the puppy for curiosity's sake.

Oversee the meeting

Exercise both dogs well before the meeting, then allow them to interact with one another, keeping a close eye to ensure that all remains calm and the meeting is positive. Toys and food can be a source of potential conflict, so pick up all your older dog's toys before the puppy arrives and make sure that you have separate toys and feeding positions for each dog.

Provide a refuge

Play pens, crates or baby gates are a good idea to use when introducing a puppy, to give your older dog some respite from the puppy and also to allow safe investigation of each other through the protection of bars. Don't leave the dogs together unsupervised for at least the first month of ownership, until you are sure that they are sound canine playmates.

▲ Children and puppies make ideal playmates so long as they are properly supervised by an adult.

MEETING CHILDREN
Give them guidelines

When you are introducing a puppy to children, always discuss the correct way of treating him beforehand so that they are not overly rough or inadvertently frightening. Explain that excited behaviour such as squealing, screaming and running about can be very scary for your new arrival and may also stimulate unwanted chasing behaviour in some puppies. Children should be dissuaded from picking up puppies, as they tend not to support them properly, resulting in discomfort and upset for the puppy. Keeping the puppy on the ground will ensure that he and the children are all comfortable and can play together in safety.

Stress his need for rest

Remind children that a puppy needs lots of sleep and tell them not to wake him up, as this will result in an irritable puppy that will not appreciate their attentions. Allow the puppy time-outs by giving him a play pen or crate in which to play or sleep on his own and consider providing a new game or hobby for the children to distract them from smothering the new arrival. After a few weeks, the novelty of a puppy tends to wear off as both puppy and children settle down to life together.

Ensure contact with kids

If you don't have any children, it is important to expose your puppy to them wherever possible. Some puppies raised in adult-only environments can find children frightening and without adequate socialization develop nervous or aggressive behaviours towards them as they grow. The high-pitched squeals of a young child combined with uncoordinated grabbing and running can not only frighten dogs but also trigger prey instincts in those not raised with them. Invite friends or family with children to interact with your puppy, or introduce him to children in the park so that his social development includes establishing relationships with young people.

INSURANCE

Why it is important

Pet insurance is fast becoming standard practice in dog ownership, with one in three canines needing veterinary treatment every year. Available from a number of different providers, pet insurance will protect you from large, unexpected veterinary bills incurred when your puppy is unwell, injured or even the cause of an accident.

Choose your policy with care

Always read policies carefully, as making a choice purely on the basis of cost may result in you falling foul of exclusions or cover limitations if your puppy should become ill. Choose a policy that provides 'cover for life', which means that the provider will continue to pay claims for ongoing conditions for the entire life of your pet. Many unscrupulous providers will stop paying claims or cancel a policy after just one year of claims for a specific condition. This may leave you without further opportunity to re-insure your pet for that illness with a competitor, as it will be classed as a pre-existing condition.

Get advice

Pet insurance generally follows the rule 'you get what you paid for', so seek advice from your vet and your dog-owning friends before making a decision about a provider.

▼ Your puppy will love the attention he gets from your children, but make sure he has plenty of time-outs too.

Regular brushing and checking of the skin also gives you the opportunity to look out for early indications of dermatological conditions, such as redness of the skin, flaky skin, loss of fur, discharge, infection, lumps or lesions, as well as external parasites such as fleas and ticks.

Nail trimming

It is important to keep your puppy's nails trimmed in the early stages, when he will be unable to wear them down naturally on walks in the outside world. You need to seek expert advice from your vet or professional groomer before attempting this at home. A blood vessel and nerve run through the centre of the nail, which can obviously bleed and cause pain if cut into. Use a pair of purpose-designed nail clippers available from a pet store or vet clinic. If you don't feel confident about doing nail trimming yourself, ask the vet clinic to show you how – many vets will offer a nail trim at the first vaccination – or visit a professional groomer.

Oral hygiene

Your puppy's baby (deciduous) teeth will fall out consistently from around three months to six months of age, when they will be replaced by adult teeth. Nevertheless, during this early period it is

GROOMING
Establish a routine

Grooming your pet is similar to the behaviour that animals perform on each other in the wild. While its primary purpose is to clean, grooming also plays a role in strengthening the bond between owner and dog. Grooming is also an opportunity to give your puppy a regular all-over health examination. Starting a grooming regime from an early age helps a puppy to accept being handled and examined before grooming becomes an essential part of his day-to-day care as he grows.

Coat care

Your puppy's fur will need brushing or combing, stripping or trimming, depending on his breed and coat condition – for example, a Border Terrier's coat is stripped, while a Poodle's is trimmed. For the more involved grooming techniques, it is best to start by visiting a professional groomer, then consider taking lessons or ask a breeder's advice as to how you can do it at home. The long-haired breeds, such as the Old English Sheepdog or Chow Chow, need to be groomed daily with a brush or comb. Brushing in the direction of hair growth will provide the most comfortable experience for your puppy.

important to introduce your puppy to teeth cleaning, so that he becomes accustomed to the procedure. This will facilitate future dental care that can prevent dental disease occurring later in life. Daily brushing is recommended, with regular checks by both owner and vet to ensure that there are no aspects of your growing puppy's dental health that need addressing. Dental disease is thought to affect around 40 per cent of dogs as early as three years of age, so purchasing and using toothbrushes, flavoured toothpastes and dental chews will keep your puppy's teeth and gums healthy and future vet bills down.

Ear cleaning

Waxy deposits can accumulate in dogs' ears – more often in dogs with floppy ears – which cause a musty odour and can lead to more serious ear infections. Get into the habit of checking your puppy's ears regularly, purchasing ear cleaners from your vet and seeking professional advice on how to use them safely. Cotton wool and liquid cleaners tend to be the most effective, but avoid cotton buds, which may inadvertently cause pain or injury to your puppy.

Bathing

Choose a mild puppy shampoo from your vet clinic or pet store and bathe your puppy by supporting his head above water and massaging in the shampoo while keeping it clear of eyes and ears. Rinse with warm water, then towel dry in a warm environment to prevent your puppy becoming cold.

Shampooing your puppy regularly can dry out his skin and strip away the coat's natural waterproofing, so only bathe him when he is dirty to a level that cannot be dealt with by brushing alone. Monthly bathing is the most frequent that a healthy coat will tolerate, although more regular bathing is required if a puppy is suffering from a skin condition. Many dogs only need bathing a few times every year.

◀ Training your puppy to allow teeth brushing is crucial for his dental health as an adult.

▲ Bathtime can be fun if your puppy is kept calm and warm. Don't over-bathe or you will strip away his coat's natural oils.

To find out more on ...

Aggression and biting, go to page 113
Animal behaviourists, go to page 117
Basic training, go to page 67
Chewing, go to page 124
First walk, go to page 80
Flea control, go to page 42
Hair loss, go to page 139
House soiling, go to page 127
Nervousness and fear, go to page 130
Poisoning, go to page 150
Tick, lice and mite control, go to page 42
Toys, go to page 25
Vaccinations, go to page 39

Weeks 8–11
The hairy toddler

This is an adorable stage when your endearing addition to the family is full of energy and enthusiasm, with many misdemeanours quickly forgotten. Be mindful that bad behaviour allowed now will only become more of a problem when he is older and bigger. So this is the time to establish good behaviour and eliminate the undesirable.

PARENTAL DUTIES

Begin socialization and training

Your puppy's keen senses will be put to full use when he arrives home, as he is bombarded by all the many sights, sounds and smells of his new environment. Just like a human toddler, your puppy will be into everything in an attempt to explore and experience the exciting new world around him. This is a very important time for your puppy's social development and the establishment of his relationship with his new family.

It is easy to get caught up in the joy and wonder of owning such a sweet and loving creature. You may fail to realize just what a crucial learning stage this is for him, which is why it is the perfect time to start basic training. Although he has a short attention span at this age, the lessons learned (either good or bad) will be difficult to modify later. This is so much the case that some believe a puppy not taught to fetch at this age, for instance, will be unable to develop the suitable skills to be a guide or detection dog later in life.

Take first housetraining steps

Both bladder and bowel control will have improved considerably from when puppy was with mum, so now it's about teaching him both when and where it is OK to go.

YOUR PUPPY'S BEHAVIOUR

Encourage exploration

Curiosity and a desire to explore are tempered by a general fear of everything, so positive encouragement of exploration will avoid possible phobias that may come to haunt your puppy in adulthood. In nature puppies of wild dogs approach unknown objects with great caution, but with subtle support provided by their mother in exploring them, they quickly come to accept them.

This measured approach to socialization is important – the balance between being overprotective and too compelling can be difficult to achieve. Don't force exposure to new things; just let it happen naturally while avoiding the temptation to over-parent, as this can lead to a fearful adult. By over-indulging your puppy with affection when he is fearful, you will only reinforce his fear. Allow him to be exposed to something long enough to either overcome his fear on his own and then investigate it or for you positively to improve the situation with treats or toys.

Assess his personality

Your puppy's individual personality will begin to shine through, so see if you can tell whether he is dominant or shy, strong-willed or eager to please. One of the joys of dog ownership is that no two dogs are ever the same. If you try to understand your dog's special character, you will gain a better appreciation of exactly what is needed to train him into a well-adjusted adult.

PAWS FOR THOUGHT
to reassure or ignore?

When human children are upset or frightened, the normal response is to hug them, talking softly to reassure them that everything is okay. We can converse verbally with other humans, enabling us to rationalize situations and overcome tears. This is not the case with your puppy. When he is frightened and you respond as you would to a child, you are giving him attention for nervous behaviour, reinforcing his reasoning that he has something to be frightened of. As pack leader, you should lead by example by being calm and relaxed, ignoring the non-threatening stimulus and your fearful dog. You should not correct or chastise your puppy either, as this will upset him further. Give him attention only when his behaviour is calm and quiet.

Desensitize your puppy to whatever is evoking the fearful response by using treats and praise as encouragement as he confronts and overcomes them. When your puppy shows greater resolve and confidence, shower him with rewards and praise to dispel irrational fears and replace them with positive feelings.

Develop his social life

Socialization with people and other dogs is essential during this life stage. Seek out puppy parties in your area until the vet says that it is safe for you to take your puppy to the park to meet older canine buddies. Invite friends and family around to meet the puppy so that he is exposed to different types and ages of people, including children. These interactions are important for the puppy not only to appreciate his place in the world but also to learn basic lessons such as control of biting, physical coordination and how to play.

WHAT YOUR PUPPY MAY DO
Behaviour that needs understanding

New owners must expect waking, crying and soiling during the night. They need to be very patient and appreciate that their puppy is still very young. Crying when left alone is common, as your puppy is unused to being separated from the affections of his owner or siblings. Fearful behaviour towards everyday objects can seem amusing, but this needs careful monitoring and understanding so that your puppy doesn't develop irrational fears and becomes a well-balanced adult dog.

◀ Encourage investigation of the 'scary vacuum monster' so that your puppy comes to accept it.

COMMON QUESTIONS
habituation

My German Shepherd puppy hates the vacuum cleaner. As soon as I turn it on, he barks, urinates and runs off. How can I help him to get used to it?

A vacuum cleaner is a frightening device to a wary puppy. It has a high-pitched whistle mixed with a low grumbling sound and lunges forward suddenly, then retreats – a very aggressive and threatening monster! Start by allowing him to explore and sniff it when it is off, placing a treat or two over the machine to encourage him to come closer. Once you can repeat this several times and your puppy is comfortable, you can attempt to turn it on while it is stationary. Follow the same process, using lots of treats and praise, then hopefully with time your puppy will be less fearful of this everyday appliance.

Behaviour that needs counteracting

Play biting and clothes pulling are something that puppies tend to indulge in and owners facilitate, but this should be dealt with quickly. Chewing is a problem at this stage while your puppy investigates his new environment. Only minor destructiveness will result, as his jaw is yet to attain full strength. Jumping up and chasing (especially other animals in the house and children) may cause alarm until your new recruit learns the rules of polite society.

WHAT YOU SHOULD DO

Feeding

Keep nutrition simple by choosing a good-quality food and sticking to it. Mixing or changing foods will upset your dog's gut, causing diarrhoea or excessive wind. Offering lots of different foods to your dog to suit his changing tastes will only lead to an over-demanding dog.

Training

Constantly remind yourself that your puppy will soon grow up, so don't allow any behaviour, such as jumping up, that may be difficult to cope with when he gets bigger. Trial the collar and lead and begin with simple commands. Above all, play with your puppy to keep training sessions fun and positive. Be a strong leader by setting house rules and keep your patience while enforcing them to correct unwanted behaviours before they become bad habits. Chewing on shoes, urinating in the house or biting overlooked at this stage may be hard to eradicate as your puppy grows older.

▲ Cuteness is no excuse for bad behaviour, such as climbing on the sofa, so set house rules and stick to them.

Family life

Watch out for disharmony in your home, as a new puppy in the house can cause jealousy between sibling children jostling for his affections. Other animals in the home can feel upset at the changes to the hierarchical structure of the family, leading to aggression or hiding. Ensure that the whole brood is carefully watched over during this hectic, disruptive time.

OLD WIVES' TAIL

You should give your puppy milk, as he is still young and misses his mum.

No, you shouldn't. Weaning is an important part of the growth process and eight-week-old puppies should be on solids by the time they leave the breeder and mum. Also, a bitch's milk is low in the carbohydrate lactose, which many puppies are intolerant to. When given cows' milk, which is high in lactose, many puppies will develop diarrhoea.

◄ Puppy parties are an opportunity for canines to socialize together in a safe, supervised environment.

Vet visits

Puppies can become very frightened of various experiences at this stage of their development and they can carry that fear with them for life. If the first appointment with your vet is traumatic, your puppy may never want to visit again (think how Betty felt with her dad being a vet!). Take food treats and a toy along with you when you visit the vet so that the rewards for going to the clinic outweigh the negatives, encouraging your puppy not to fear these necessary visits in the future.

Preventative treatments

Vaccinations are due at eight weeks and then again at between 10 and 12 weeks, depending on the product used by your vet. Worming medication should be given every fortnight at this age. If your puppy is going into your garden, it is a good idea to administer a flea treatment. You can obtain a topical flea treatment suitable for your puppy's weight from the vet.

Social development

Avoid startling your puppy – from eight to ten weeks of age they are very prone to developing fear, so keep all new experiences positive and non-threatening. Attend a puppy party in your local area, which are great fun and highly educational for both you and your puppy. Socializing with other dogs and people is very important, so don't just sit at home enjoying your beautiful new playmate on your own. Organize play dates with other puppies, have friends around, take your puppy out in the car and expose him to everyday life.

HEALTH REMINDERS

Safety precautions

During this time your puppy must be kept in safe environments (for example, the home, garden and vet clinic). Avoid exposure to other possibly unvaccinated dogs until at least a few days after his second vaccination (around 10 to 12 weeks). This is because your puppy does not develop an active immunity to the diseases protected against after the first vaccination. To achieve active immunity, he needs the booster vaccination.

PAWS FOR THOUGHT
to pick up or not?

If your puppy is in obvious danger, picking him up is appropriate. In all other cases, allow your puppy the chance to assess the situation for himself and often the initial fear reaction will be replaced by interest . . . followed by boredom! For example, picking up a puppy that quivers when meeting a friendly child is not a good idea, as cuddling him during this time may reinforce the idea that he has something to be nervous about. Instead, divert his attention with a toy while getting the child to stroke him using soothing tones or offering a treat.

Health problems

Diarrhoea is common in the early stages of puppy ownership due to diet alterations. Your puppy's gut has to become accustomed to new foods and the stress of changes in his environment. If the diarrhoea persists for more than 24 hours or there is any blood or worms present, contact your vet.

Microchipping and insurance

Microchip and insure your puppy for his protection and your peace of mind.

BASIC TRAINING AT HOME

Rewards of early training

Even at the tender age of eight weeks, your puppy is an eager student waiting to be taught the finer points of life with humans. Basic training is a great way to communicate with your puppy, fostering a sense of himself and his place in the world. Training will enhance your relationship with your puppy, establish good habits early to give structure and boundaries to his new environment and avoid the development of undesirable behaviours that may be difficult to modify later. Training results in a grown dog that will be calm, well behaved in all situations and safe, responding quickly to commands.

Rules of engagement

Follow this checklist of basic rules to govern all your interactions with your puppy:

- ☐ **Be consistent** – start with a strict set of house rules and stick to them.
- ☐ **Be patient** – your young puppy has a limited attention span, so lessons need to be short and frequent.
- ☐ **Be positive** – give excessive amounts of praise when your puppy does the right thing.
- ☐ **Be fair** – accept that mistakes and accidents will happen; never resort to physical punishment.
- ☐ **Be rational** – accept that you are human and will make mistakes, lose your temper and wonder what you have done wrong. Every puppy parent feels the same at some point, so ask for help or take a break and soon these feelings will pass.

▲ Giving lots of love and praise is the best way to treat a puppy who behaves well.

Training principles

Puppy training must always be kept short and interesting, using simple commands starting with your puppy's name. Have treats and lots of attention at the ready to reward the puppy when he does something right. Do not repeat commands more than a few times, as they will become noise without meaning. Avoid giving commands in harsh tones, as this will decrease the likelihood of your puppy responding to them.

To reinforce the training, assign a hand gesture to go with each command. Trainers have varying hand gestures for different commands, so it really doesn't matter which one you use as long as you are consistent. To avoid confusing your puppy, make sure that the whole family uses the same gestures and verbal commands. Getting all members of the household to practise the simple training exercises on pages 68–71 at different times of the day for just a few minutes each time is key to achieving the best results.

BASIC TRAINING EXERCISES

At this age you can begin to teach your puppy basic skills, such as walking on a lead, come, sit and stay, as well as the 'good dog' and 'no' commands. With time and patience, these can be fine-tuned to allow your grown puppy to compete in obedience trials, sporting competitions and other doggy pursuits.

Come!

1 Using your puppy's name, crouch down with open arms and call him to you. As you do so, you can offer a treat as an enticement.

2 When he comes, hold his collar, then reward him with lots of affection and the treat. In your garden use other family members or friends to restrain him, calling him to you from greater distances to test his responses both on and off the lead.

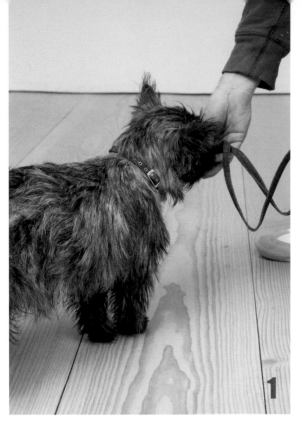

Walking on a lead

1 Before you start venturing out into the park, your puppy should have been exposed to the lead at home. Burn up some excess puppy energy with an active game, then offer your puppy the chance to sniff and examine the lead before attaching it to his collar.

2 Keeping your puppy's attention on you and not the collar by using a treat, ask him to come with you, ensuring that you keep the lead slack. If he pulls, immediately stop and call the puppy back to you so that he quickly realizes that pulling on the lead doesn't get him anywhere. Don't allow chewing of the lead when walking, as this annoying habit can lead to dominance problems in your puppy later.

Sit!

1 Gaining your puppy's attention with a treat, get him to come close while looking up at you. Keep hold of the treat and let his nose touch it, then slowly move it up and back over his head towards his tail. If his front legs remain on the ground, he should naturally sit as his back end sinks towards the ground.

2 Say your puppy's name and 'sit' as his bottom touches the ground, then reward him with the treat and lots of fuss. If he stands up on his back legs or moves backwards, you may be moving the treat too high or fast. Later, progress to using a hand gesture, rewarding your puppy when he sits by crouching down and giving him attention or a tasty morsel.

1

2

Stay!

1 With your puppy in the sit position, stay close to him and say his name and the 'stay' command. Keep still to prevent him confusing your movements with a command to move and reward him if he remains in place for ten seconds. With practice, gradually increase the time period in the sit position and try to make slow, deliberate movements away from your puppy while still facing him. If he remains in place, then return to him and treat, gradually increasing the 'stay' time and the distance moved away.

BETTY'S DIARY
mutual mistakes

Day 2 Night two was worse than night one – I paid for my soft stance of going to see her during the previous night, as she wailed with even greater intensity for the first three hours. I had to go in and clean her up, as she was covered in faeces, but she failed to stop wailing for more than two hours. Feeling like I had been through a washing machine, I woke very early and when she had just a tiny break of vocalization I got her out of her cage. It was very hard to follow strict rules of night-time treatment, as once she was awake and out the cage she needed constant supervision or my house would be one big walk-in toilet. Unfortunately, sleep deprivation got the better of me and I again crumbled, inviting Betty into bed for a morning cuddle and some peace!

Day 3 Betty was not about to abate her bad behaviour, defecating on the rug in the living room and then urinating on her bed. Both times I caught her in the act, but it was too late to deposit her on her training pads. I removed anything furry or fluffy from the room besides the training pads, which I surrounded in towels in the hope that she would begin to use them. I decided to make mealtimes a more regimented affair on the basis that feeding her late at night would mean that hunger wouldn't be one of the reasons she would wake. Just as tired as me, Betty slept much of the day at my feet and it was very difficult to be mad at such an adorable creature that just wanted to be near. I tried to keep her awake before bedtime to save her slumber for when I went to bed. She did surprise me by using the training pad for the first time – I took a photo!

During the night, I made a steadfast decision not to go in to her and not to let her sleep in my bed on waking up. Initially she again wailed, this time throwing in the sound of a stuck pig (high-pitched sounds are commonly noted by owners nearing success!), which made me fear for her wellbeing. She soon calmed down and gave me six hours of blissful uninterrupted sleep before again waking me with whining. I went in to see her only when there was a gap between the whines so that she didn't think that it was the whining that had made me come.

Lessons learned
Listen to my own advice (be tough) and try to bring a puppy home over the weekend or at a time when sleep deprivation is not so important!

'Good dog' versus 'no'

1 Teaching the meaning of these two most common utterances heard by your puppy is a vital lesson. Position yourself and a friend or family member opposite each other and about 3 metres (10 feet) apart. Call your puppy and give him the 'sit' command. When he responds correctly, give him the verbal reward 'good dog' – spoken in a high-pitched voice that your puppy associates with excitement – and a treat.

2 Then deliberately turn away from him and say a quiet 'no' – best delivered with a subtle growl in your voice, which the puppy will recognize as a sound of disapproval from his time with his mother and siblings. Actively starve him of attention to reinforce that the word 'no' means a loss of privilege. Then the other person should call the puppy and the exercise can continue for a few minutes. Use 'no' and the action of turning away to correct your puppy consistently, rather than raising your voice, which can frighten him and any children present.

8–11 WEEKS: OWNER CHECKLISTS

What your puppy may do

- [ ] Night-time waking, crying and soiling
- [ ] House soiling
- [ ] Play biting and clothes pulling
- [ ] Chewing and minor destructiveness
- [ ] Chasing of other animals and children
- [ ] Crying when left alone
- [ ] Jumping up
- [ ] Being fearful of everyday objects around the home

What you should do

- [ ] Set house rules from the start and stick to them
- [ ] Be a strong, fair leader
- [ ] Start basic training and play with your puppy
- [ ] Keep nutrition simple
- [ ] Avoid startling your puppy or comforting him when fearful
- [ ] Attend a puppy party
- [ ] Socialize your puppy with different types of people

Health reminders

- [ ] Keep your puppy in a hygienic environment
- [ ] Vaccinations are due at 8 weeks and then at 10–12 weeks
- [ ] Give a worming treatment fortnightly
- [ ] Apply a topical flea treatment
- [ ] Microchip and insure your puppy

To find out more on . . .

Aggression and biting, go to page 113

Chewing, go to page 124

Collars and leads, go to page 26

Flea control, go to page 42

Food, go to page 27

House soiling, go to page 127

Insurance, go to page 59

Microchipping, go to page 43

Nervousness and fear, go to page 130

Over-excitement, go to page 118

Puppy parties, go to page 38

Socialization and habituation, go to page 55

Toilet training, go to page 46

Vaccinations, go to page 39

Visiting the vet, go to page 37

Worming, go to page 40

Weeks 12–15
The juvenile delinquent

Finally your puppy can venture into the great outdoors and expend some of that boundless energy. Many trainers believe that this stage is key for owners to establish good behaviour and self-confidence in their charges. With the 'cute factor' wearing off over toileting mishaps and chewed belongings, your puppy will begin to challenge you, so be prepared for some patient parenting.

▲ Exposing your puppy early to the sights and sounds of the great outdoors helps ensure a well-behaved adult dog.

PARENTAL DUTIES
His guide to the outside world

Once the vaccination course has been completed, the job of exposing your puppy to the amazing and potentially frightening outside world begins. This major event may bring an increase in behavioural problems such as fear and aggression. All the socialization and habituation completed indoors must be moved outdoors with greater intensity and variation. Gradually, your puppy should be given the opportunity to experience the sights and sounds of motor vehicles, crowds and other dogs.

YOUR PUPPY'S BEHAVIOUR
Prepare to be challenged

Your puppy will start to test you, questioning your authority and asserting his dominance. Some puppies may show stubbornness or aggression in the process of clarifying their place in the hierarchy of your pack, while others will more readily accept their low status. A structured home life with strong leadership, routine and strict rules will ensure a relatively painless transition through this period.

Avoid playing rough games that teach your puppy to challenge or even bite you, as you are not his sibling or equal but his superior whom he should never challenge. At this stage you must appreciate that although early signs of aggression may not be as dangerous as in an adult dog, you should implement a zero-tolerance policy now to avoid worrying behaviours becoming the norm.

Prepare for backsliding in training

Your previous good work on the training front may seem to be going backwards, as your puppy enjoys his independence and selectively ignores commands. With all the captivating smells, sights and sounds of the outdoors combined with their newfound freedom, puppies of this age need gentle but firm reinforcement of commands and training to ensure that they are kept in line. It is worth considering enrolling in training classes at this stage (see page 82), which offer advanced training lessons designed to stimulate your puppy and underline the message that you are boss.

PAWS FOR THOUGHT
playing rough

Many owners, especially males, like to play rough with their charges, thinking that this is just another entertaining game that will 'toughen up' their puppy. This type of activity may seem fun to us, but constant physical tussles can teach your puppy to challenge you. In the wild, just a growl from a dominant dog will avert an altercation with a rival, without the need for a physical fight. When you play rough or a tug-of-war game, your puppy sets himself against you in a battle of will and strength, which spawns questions as to who is the most dominant. It also provides him with an opportunity to dominate, sometimes extending to mouthing and biting. Even the softest of bites should be swiftly dealt with, as no bite would be tolerated from a subordinate in a pack situation. A firm, low-growled 'no' should be uttered immediately, followed by a period of starving your puppy of attention to dissuade him from this potentially dangerous behaviour.

It does seem as though the early stages of puppy training are all about what you can't do with your puppy, like in an army boot camp. But time will reveal that lessons learned early within a strictly developed social structure result in an obedient adult dog that is able to experience more of what the world has to offer than if he were unruly.

WHAT YOUR PUPPY MAY DO
Behaviour that needs understanding
Some lucky owners will already be enjoying a fully housetrained puppy, but occasional accidents are generally still to be expected indoors.

In his new encounters with the outside world, your puppy may show fearful tendencies in the form of wariness of strangers, children, crowds, traffic noise and other dogs. If you are unlucky or do not manage to read the warning signs, your puppy may also become a victim of canine aggression outdoors.

Behaviour that needs counteracting
Destructiveness is common at this age, with your puppy becoming stronger, taller and able to reach a whole new variety of playthings. His increased activity and energy levels can lead to boisterousness, chasing and aggressive play fighting with children and other animals. He may begin to question your authority, ignoring you or barking when given commands or growling at you

▼ Occasional housetraining accidents are still to be expected at this stage of development.

when playing with toys. You are not the only one whose frustration levels may rise – other animals in your household may also show signs of irritability and stress as a result of the new arrival.

WHAT YOU SHOULD DO

Housetraining strategies

Be patient with persistent house-wetters and avoid cleaning up in front of him. Angry body language is easily detectable by your puppy and will result in him finding more obscure places to toilet indoors.

If he is successfully using training pads at this stage, decrease their use or remove them completely to encourage a greater confidence in toileting outdoors. A common mistake is to cosset a puppy in continuing to allow him to toilet only indoors without actively teaching him to go outside. Limiting a puppy to one toileting spot and one medium, such as a training pad, up until the end of this period will result in his resistance to the use of others, for example grass or flower beds. If your puppy is solely conditioned to associate going to the toilet with being inside on a training pad, even when taken for a long walk outdoors he may hold on until he finds himself back indoors on familiar territory.

Simply having a garden and leaving the door open doesn't mean that your puppy will learn to use the outside rather than going indoors. Put him on a lead and walk him outside, spending time with him so that you are there to reward him with treats and praise when he goes.

If he is still making multiple daily mistakes, keep as calm as you can and take positive action. Put yourself constantly on 'wee watch', monitoring your puppy's habits to gain an understanding of when he toilets (such as after drinking or before bedtime), so that you can devise an effective toileting timetable. Actively walk your puppy outside or place him on his training pads during those regular toileting times in an attempt to give him the ability to go correctly in the right spot. Always remember to reinforce the action positively with treats and praise, to ensure that the lesson is well learned by the puppy.

▲ Walking your puppy outdoors after a meal gives you the chance to praise him for toileting outside.

Outings and social development

Never feel embarrassed to ask owners of fully grown dogs if their pet is aggressive towards other dogs before you allow your puppy to interact with them. If your puppy is getting over-excited or you are concerned about the possibility of aggression, extricate them from the situation using lead pressure and verbal commands. Reward your puppy when he comes to you with treats and attention to finish on a positive note. Remind yourself of canine body language to help avoid potentially calamitous dog encounters.

Conversely, don't smother your puppy – remember that he is a dog and needs to learn about the world. If you don't give him some freedom at this stage, your puppy may be fearful or shy for the rest of his life. Walks are also important in teaching him to accept being on the lead.

Don't forget other members of the family. Give any other dogs or cats the adequate attention they deserve in order to avoid jealousy or aggression. Consider keeping your puppy restricted to certain parts of the house at times so that the other animals can get some peace.

PAWS FOR THOUGHT
training people

One thing I noticed during Betty's training was that in some respects she would behave for me and not for others. I was reminded of the way most people are unwilling to reprimand naughty children when their parents are near by. This human trait seems to hold true when applied to other people's dogs: a visitor to your home will be reticent about scolding a misbehaving puppy when you are present, so in most cases you do the reprimanding for them, which does not work as well as if they had done it themselves.

This is a complicated social situation, as dogs are pack animals, needing instruction from all members of the group to appreciate their lowly status at the bottom of the hierarchical ladder. Betty jumping up was a terrible problem with visitors, although I quickly taught her that she would gain no attention when jumping up to me. Visitors would let her do so, however, and even actively encourage it, not appreciating that jumping up is a bad habit. My reprimands to get down then fell on deaf ears.

Be prepared to impart your knowledge to others so that your puppy receives the consistency of instruction he needs. Make sure everyone uses a command such as 'down' or 'no'. Most importantly, when your puppy performs the correct response for guests, encourage them to reinforce the lesson with lots of praise or a treat.

▶ Teach visitors to ignore a jumping puppy, only giving him affection when he is on all four feet.

Training

Consider enrolling in training classes during this stage to challenge your developing puppy (see page 82). You should also keep training him using basic commands at home, both indoors and outdoors. Begin teaching your puppy that life with humans involves some separation. This is an important lesson, similar to the one children learn when they discover that going to school involves being away from their parents for periods of time. Begin training him to be on his own by leaving him for short periods in secure places of the house, such as in his own play pen, enriched with toys. Get your puppy used to being separated from you for short lengths of time while you are at home, gradually extending the time up to one hour.

HEALTH REMINDERS

Preventative treatments

Monthly worming until six months of age is recommended using liquids or pastes for smaller puppies and tablets for larger ones. Apply a flea treatment monthly to avoid any flea allergies developing. Ensure that it is administered at least 48 hours after bathing, as most treatments require a healthy amount of sweat present on the skin to be effectively absorbed.

Health checks and routines

Check between toes and in the eyes and ears for foreign bodies such as grass seeds and twigs – a puppy isn't adept at removing them on his own.

Diarrhoea can be a problem at this stage too, now caused by eating undesirable items in the park. Be vigilant and learn which parks have the least amount of scraps left lying around.

Your puppy will begin teething now, so provide him with lots of interesting toys to chew to help alleviate the discomfort.

Consider giving your puppy his first bathing or grooming session, plucking his ears if need be to keep them clean and clear.

▶ Check between the toes of your puppy after walks to remove foreign bodies and identify any injuries early.

COMMON QUESTION
pet passports

Do I still need to get a rabies vaccination for my puppy's pet passport if he is travelling to a country that doesn't have rabies?

Yes. Even in the case of travelling between countries such as the UK and Australia, where rabies is not found, your dog will still require a rabies vaccination, then a blood test. The rationale behind this is that the dog may transit through countries that are not rabies free, so the rule of vaccinating for rabies is universal for all international travel under the pet passport scheme.

Microchipping

If your puppy hasn't yet been microchipped, do it at this stage before he starts leaving the safety of your house and garden.

Travel requirements

If you are interested in travelling abroad with your puppy, get his first rabies vaccination completed after he is 12 weeks of age.

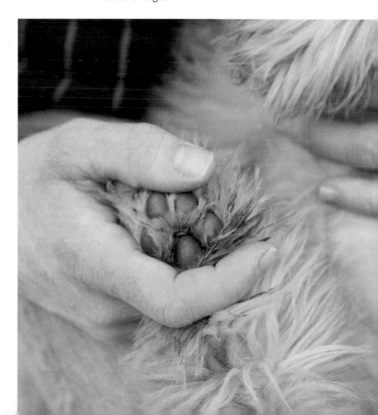

◀ Exploring the park for the first time will be very
exciting for your puppy – expect him to be thorough!

experience or meeting involving aggression is
worse than no meeting at all.

Possessing a basic knowledge of canine body
language will allow you to preside safely over the
first walk and to avert any unwelcome incidents.
Initial nerves or fears are understandable responses
in your puppy on this big day, which can physically
manifest as barking, hiding, freezing, trembling or
holding his tail between his legs. Allow your puppy
the chance to overcome his nervousness without
your intervention, as prior knowledge will tell you
that, given a few moments to assess the situation,
a puppy tends to shed his nerves and assume a
more robust attitude.

Always keep your puppy on a collar, halter or
harness and lead, as it is preferable that your
puppy is restricted rather than being able to run
away from you in excitement or fear. A long or
extendible lead will give him freedom to explore
while keeping him within your control.

PARK LIFE
Make it mutually enjoyable

As a puppy owner, you will develop a new
appreciation of local parks as your puppy is allowed
to venture forth into the outside world. During this
exploration, you will expose him to many potentially
frightening experiences, including new environments,
dogs and strangers. With common sense prevailing,
most fear-evoking scenarios can be comfortably
negotiated, resulting in you both being able to enjoy
your outings in the park.

The first walk

A long-awaited event in most new-dog households,
walking your puppy outside in public for the first
time is an exciting experience for all. It is highly
rewarding to watch your puppy's reactions to things
and to show off the latest addition to your family
with parental pride. Your puppy will be experiencing
so much for the first time, so it is your job to ensure
that all these experiences are positive. A negative

▶ Crouch down to offer comfort and protection when your puppy meets other dogs for the first time.

Meeting other dogs

Making friends with other canines is important for your puppy in order to learn dog etiquette, so that he doesn't develop fear-related aggression and isn't perturbed by the variation in canine size and shape. Ask the owners if their dogs are friendly with other dogs before allowing your puppy to get close. Don't assume that all big dogs can't be trusted, as it is more likely that your puppy will be attacked by a dog of similar size and stature than an obviously larger, more dominant adult.

Place your puppy on the ground with lead attached and crouch down to allow him to retreat beneath you while you gently ward off the other dog, reinforcing your position as protector and pack leader. When your puppy seems ready, tell the owner to let the other dog approach on the lead.

▼ Strangers should approach slowly and offer a hand to be sniffed before stroking your puppy.

Meeting other people

People generally love puppies and will be eager to meet your adorable young charge when you are in the park. Although it is important to expose him to all the shapes, sizes and ages of other humans, early meetings should be calm and gradual.

Ask any strangers who want to meet your puppy to approach slowly, allowing the puppy to sniff their hand before stroking. If your puppy seems nervous, request that they don't stare directly at him. Direct eye contact in the wild is challenging, so it can be a little threatening to your puppy. Most maturing puppies will overcome this perception, realizing that humans look each other in the eye without wishing to engage in conflict. This can be achieved at home by giving your puppy a treat while looking him in the eye and smiling. If you use this approach, he will gradually begin to recognize the range of human facial expressions that are associated with positive or non-threatening emotions.

PUPPY TRAINING CLASSES

How they will help

Training classes are fun, informative and rewarding experiences for both you and your growing puppy. They vary greatly in structure, style and content, although obedience training is the most common type. As well as training puppies, they are equally designed to train new owners, who are usually the ones responsible for the failings of their charges in the first place, due to poor canine understanding. Classes will also help to address and correct any behavioural problems that you may be concerned about (see Problem solver, pages 112–135).

▲ Socialization with other dogs is a very important aspect of puppy training classes.

Choosing a class

Ask the advice of other dog owners and your vet to find one that is reputable, even attending a few different classes without your puppy to choose the best one. Small classes of no more than ten puppies, in which the participants remain the same every week to ensure consistency of training, are the most effective. Puppies should also be of similar size and age for socialization exercises to be most beneficial for all involved.

BETTY'S DIARY
our first argument

Day 40 Betty has just grown tall enough to jump onto my expensive leather couch. However cute it is to see her ambitions finally realized, I swiftly condemned her actions and told her to get off. For the first time in our relationship and in true tantrum style, she began to bark at me. I replied with a firm 'no', only to be peppered with little testing barks and scampering theatrics. My first reaction was one of amusement, though putting my dog training hat quickly on, I appreciated that this was the first sign of rebellion that needed to be quickly quelled. I again retorted 'no', then, holding her collar, walked Betty into her crate, where she remained for five minutes. I released her in silence, then gave her attention when she sat on command a minute later, things calmly returning to normal.

Day 41 Repeat offender! I left Betty for a few minutes to go and get some milk at the local shop. When I returned she was laying resplendent on the sofa, chewing a sheepskin cushion with the smug satisfaction of a juvenile delinquent. 'Get down!' I thundered and she leapt off the couch at pace. I then sat down to examine the saliva-stained cushion, when again she started to bark at me. 'No,' I demanded, but she continued to bark and leap about. I repeated myself, but to no avail, and she was returned to the crate for a well-deserved time out. I realized that she was feeding off my annoyance by barking louder and at higher pitches, so swore to myself that next time, one 'get down' and the correct response in Betty would be the end of it. Later that afternoon she again perpetrated the unthinkable, launching herself onto the couch. I countered with a formulaic 'get down,' which to her credit she did. Betty then started with the barking again, but this time I ignored her, as I appreciated that I had exerted my dominance by sitting on the couch she had been banished from and within a short time she retired to her bed to sulk in silent defeat.

Lesson learned
Patience, consistency and understanding your puppy's individuality are crucial in order to maintain a calm household.

Undesirable training methods

Avoid any class that uses force or punishment as a quick-fix solution. This type of aversion therapy may get an immediate result, but will lead to behavioural problems in your puppy later in life.

Socialization stage

After choosing a class that meets your needs and suits your lifestyle, arrive early to allow your puppy to settle after his car journey. Astute trainers will assess each puppy that joins the class and determine its needs based on temperament. A good dog trainer tailors the class to suit the character and disposition of each puppy-and-owner pairing. Most classes begin with a play period during which the puppies are allowed to socialize together under the watchful eye of the trainer. Any excessive force or aggression will be quickly quelled by the trainer to avoid fearful responses and to keep proceedings positive.

▼ Don't give your puppy mixed messages. If you don't want him on the sofa, keep him off at all times.

Training strategies

The next step is the demonstration of basic commands by the trainer with each puppy, at times rather annoyingly gaining a quick response to a command that has previously brought you little success. Most training strategies involve understanding your puppy's point of view in a given situation and responding accordingly to affirm the positive response.

How you can benefit

Your trainer will have an excellent understanding of canine behaviour and body language and will be able to use this knowledge to train a puppy to do what they want when they want it. As the weeks pass, the classes will teach you these skills and give you the opportunity to ask questions in a supportive environment to improve your understanding of the canine mind. A training programme will generally be given to you as you leave, with at-home exercises and owner tuition designed to help you mould your growing puppy into a calm, well-behaved adult.

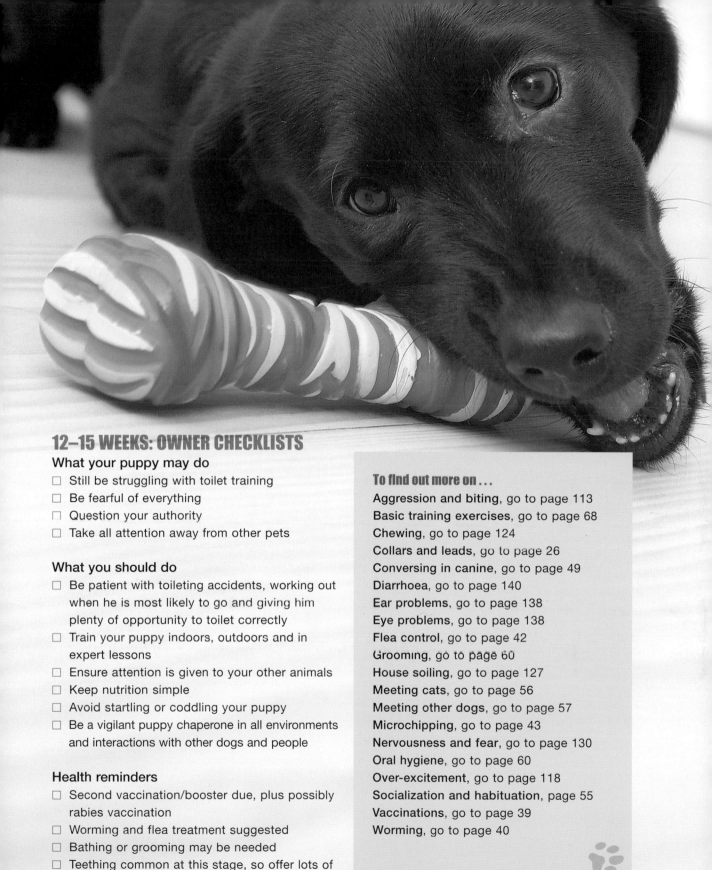

12–15 WEEKS: OWNER CHECKLISTS

What your puppy may do
- ☐ Still be struggling with toilet training
- ☐ Be fearful of everything
- ☐ Question your authority
- ☐ Take all attention away from other pets

What you should do
- ☐ Be patient with toileting accidents, working out when he is most likely to go and giving him plenty of opportunity to toilet correctly
- ☐ Train your puppy indoors, outdoors and in expert lessons
- ☐ Ensure attention is given to your other animals
- ☐ Keep nutrition simple
- ☐ Avoid startling or coddling your puppy
- ☐ Be a vigilant puppy chaperone in all environments and interactions with other dogs and people

Health reminders
- ☐ Second vaccination/booster due, plus possibly rabies vaccination
- ☐ Worming and flea treatment suggested
- ☐ Bathing or grooming may be needed
- ☐ Teething common at this stage, so offer lots of toys to avoid chewing of belongings

To find out more on . . .

Aggression and biting, go to page 113
Basic training exercises, go to page 68
Chewing, go to page 124
Collars and leads, go to page 26
Conversing in canine, go to page 49
Diarrhoea, go to page 140
Ear problems, go to page 138
Eye problems, go to page 138
Flea control, go to page 42
Grooming, go to page 60
House soiling, go to page 127
Meeting cats, go to page 56
Meeting other dogs, go to page 57
Microchipping, go to page 43
Nervousness and fear, go to page 130
Oral hygiene, go to page 60
Over-excitement, go to page 118
Socialization and habituation, page 55
Vaccinations, go to page 39
Worming, go to page 40

Weeks 16–19

Teenage rebellion

This period sees all the attributes of a teenager come to the fore. Willingness to run from authority, experimenting with stealing and exhibiting antisocial behaviour, poor manners and selective deafness can make you question your decision to get a dog. Consistency is the key to success, with skills learned in the past being heavily called upon to survive this trying period.

PARENTAL DUTIES

Be vigilant in monitoring behaviour

A strong bond will have developed between you and your puppy by this age, helping to bring problems under control with patience, understanding and love. Having jumped many behavioural and training hurdles to get here, you should not become complacent. With his self-confidence increasing, your puppy will not be so eager to please, resulting in a battle of wills that can last many months. More complicated behavioural problems may just begin to manifest themselves and must be addressed swiftly, otherwise your puppy (and you) may be destined to live with them forever.

Be persistent in his development

Akin to human teenagers, your puppy may not appreciate being restrained, cuddled or groomed at this stage, but it is important that you persist in your efforts to ensure that he will allow these practices to continue in the future.

YOUR PUPPY'S BEHAVIOUR

Prepare for volatility

Your puppy can exhibit a distinct duality of character at this stage, being sweet, well-trained and attentive one minute and then crazed and ignorant the next. Although your puppy would like you to believe that he is an adult, he is far from it. Understanding this, you need to keep your puppy well under control to avoid actual bodily harm, while allowing him enough freedom to make mistakes and learn from them.

Re-assess his personality

Your puppy's personality is being fine-tuned now; displays of increased shyness or over-exuberant boisterousness are aspects of behaviour that need addressing. It will become obvious whether your puppy is dominant or subordinate by nature, with each personality type bringing with it both positive and negative attributes. Dominance or nervous, fearful aggression may have reared its ugly head, which can fill an owner with despair.

▲ A naughty puppy may be less amusing when household chores need to be done.

The breed of your puppy will begin to have its effect on his personality, with the genetic heritage of the working role for which his ancestors were specifically bred resulting in both interesting antics and behavioural conundrums in the home environment. More complex training can be attempted to channel newfound independence or skills, tailoring this to suit the particular attributes of the student, while avoiding any under-valuing of house rules or respect for elders.

Watch out for fearfulness

Fear can again be evident in this month of life, with your puppy harbouring the desire to run from any real or perceived threats that he encounters. Maintaining the balance between continued exposure to new individuals and environments and protection from fear-related situations can be challenging. Don't be afraid to seek out experts in the fields of behaviour, training and veterinary medicine to ensure that any difficult behaviours exhibited at this stage are dealt with correctly.

WHAT YOUR PUPPY MAY DO

Declare his allegiance

Despite all your teenage puppy's rebellious behaviour, he will show an obvious bond with you and your family, which somehow manages to cancel out all the bad points.

Behaviour that needs understanding

Your puppy may exhibit new fears of things he has been exposed to previously, with fear of traffic, new environments and a nervousness around strangers added to the mix. He may start to resent being groomed or examined and still have the occasional toileting accident indoors. Chewing should be on the decrease, although your puppy will become bored of old toys and increasingly destructive if they are not regularly substituted for new ones.

▼ Chewing his lead can be the teenage puppy's way of rebelling against authority.

Behaviour that needs counteracting

Your puppy may experiment with ever more elaborate ways to break the rules in your presence and may also misbehave when he is left alone. Barking, destructiveness and soiling can all be early warning signs of over-attachment or separation anxiety disorders that can plague your puppy into adulthood. Biting of the lead, other people, animals and even you may occur during this testing period. These behaviours need to be corrected immediately.

Some puppies will have been trusted off the lead in the park with mixed results – many will run off scavenging for any discarded edible morsels, appearing as though they have been deprived of proper meals! With growing stature and self-confidence, your puppy may begin stealing food from plates or develop mild food-related aggressive tendencies towards other animals or people, including you.

WHAT YOU SHOULD DO
Day-to-day discipline

Continue to be a good leader by exhibiting fairness and consistency. Don't let your attention to training and house rules wane and start allowing your puppy to commit minor misdemeanours. Ensure that all members of the house are following the same rule book, as different rules from different people will confuse him and reignite questions of dominance. Never allow biting or aggression. Be sure to discuss any such problems that you are having with your puppy with other family members to vent frustration and keep tension and annoyance levels down within the household.

Keep a close eye on the problem if you have seen any evidence of aggression or nervousness in your puppy. If the situation appears to be worsening, talk to your vet regarding possible referral for specialist behavioural advice.

▲ Consistent ownership, with everyone in the family following the same rules, will be rewarded with a well-behaved puppy.

COMMON QUESTIONS
behaviour

When my puppy really misbehaves badly, is it OK to give him a sharp smack across his hindquarters or nose to make him understand how naughty he's been?

Physical punishment should *never* be used. Physically reprimanding a puppy to teach it discipline is an archaic method still used by some today. However, behaving in this way will only break the bond of trust and friendship that you have developed with your puppy, leading to a fearful individual that may develop aggressive tendencies towards you or others in the future.

It is hard to use restraint in the heat of the moment, but always pause for a few seconds to think about the situation and respond in a calm, appropriate way to avoid undoing all your good work and potentially scarring your puppy for life. In most cases, physical punishment will teach a dog nothing more than how to avoid being hit in the future – it will continue to behave badly, but avoiding you.

A type of physical punishment that was commonly used in the past is 'rubbing a puppy's nose in it' when it has inappropriately urinated or defecated indoors. This reaction will simply frighten your puppy, although occasionally it can result in a puppy developing a taste for faeces! Be honest with yourself and know your limitations; if you have had a testing day or feel that your patience is low, keep training to a minimum by providing your puppy with appropriate chew toys and treats to facilitate a relaxed, carefree evening.

◀ Teaching tricks, such as 'sit up and beg', is a great way to stimulate a growing puppy.

Training

Train your puppy to be left for up to a period of three hours. Selectively ignore him for 15 minutes before you leave and provide toys, food and water in a secure and temperate part of the home. Take longer and more interesting walks now that your puppy is calmer and better behaved on the lead. Continue with training classes and home lessons, such as teaching tricks.

You can also learn more about your particular breed of dog, finding out what they were originally bred for and like to do, so that you can nurture their inherent abilities. For example, the Border Collie is a herding dog, so will be very good at fetch and other hide-and-seek games. You can even try teaching this breed to dance, since it requires good agility, another excellent ability of a Border Collie.

To lead or not to lead?

There comes a time in any young puppy's life when you have to let him off the lead. The timing of this event is a point of much debate and greatly depends on your puppy's individual development and your training regimen. A lead is the only thing that stands between your puppy and potential danger, so it must remain in place until you are certain that his responses to commands are reliable or the environment that you release him in is safe and secure.

If in doubt try a long lead, which will give your puppy a sense of freedom and provide a life line if he proves himself unworthy. In areas free of entanglements, such as a field with no dogs or other animals, children or elderly people around, these leads can be used to test out basic commands when your puppy is nearing readiness to be let off lead. Make a point of being animated on walks so that you are the most interesting attraction in the park, using treats and praise to guarantee your puppy's quick return to you. Continue practising basic commands at home and in the garden to hone his recall skills, trialling him off the lead outdoors when there is nothing obvious around to divert his attention away from you.

▼ Only consider off-lead adventures when you are sure that your puppy responds well to your commands.

BETTY'S DIARY
terror and the terrier

Day 79 I was working at a veterinary clinic beside a huge field, so in my lunch break I took the very excited Betty for a walk there. She was a fetch legend at this stage (having shown early signs of prowess on her very first day at home). I found myself to be the only dog owner in sight so, distancing myself from the road and entrance, I let Betty off the lead. I threw the ball numerous times, Betty returning it, dropping it and receiving a treat for her good work.

I then allowed her to sniff around on her own, as I noticed three young boys walking back from the tennis courts on the far side of the field. As they were walking straight for us and Betty was close and otherwise amused, I left her off the lead. Betty then trotted up very slowly and in ultra-cute style to say hello. Two of the boys came to greet her, but the other was slightly more reticent. I enthused that she was just a puppy and was very friendly, but he kept his distance.

After getting a fuss from the other boys, Betty approached the other boy, hoping for more of the same. The boy then suddenly took flight, running off in a farcical escape from this terrifying puppy. As Betty is a Border Terrier, a group of dogs bred for chasing, this was the beginning of a nightmare. She set off at pace to catch up with this gameful stranger, barking with delight and ignoring my commands to come. The boy was heading straight for the open gate and the road outside, but luckily I am a regular jogger and managed to cut him off, yelling for him to stop. Betty then immediately stopped, looking up at the boy and me to see where the next game would come from.

With harsh words spoken and lead put on, I asked Betty to sit and gave her a treat before returning to work for a lie down and some heart medication!

Lessons learned
Remain vigilant in parks. Friendly dogs can make us complacent when it comes to meeting people, so always chaperone any interaction to avoid frightening situations occurring for you, other people or your puppy.

▲ Keep your growing puppy stimulated with interesting new walks and novel toys.

HEALTH REMINDERS

Preventative treatments

Worming is again due this month, with most puppies now large enough to move on to tablet wormers. Flea-control application is important, especially at this stage when your puppy is venturing further afield outdoors.

Health checks and routines

Continue to examine your puppy in general, so that any issues such as skin problems, parasites and eye and ear infections can be identified early on and treated or prevented. Grooming, teeth brushing and bathing are practical ways to give your dog a regular, all-over check. Keeping him familiar with these procedures at home will make it less stressful when you visit the vet.

Check his ear canals for wax build-up and foreign bodies. Liquid cleaners can be obtained from your vet to keep your puppy's ears looking and smelling clean.

Your puppy's nails may have grown long enough to injure you or be pulled out and cause him pain. Walking on roughened surfaces such as cement footpaths is the best way to keep his nails short. Check them regularly and if necessary trim them or get them professionally manicured.

You may notice some teeth falling out, but don't worry, these are baby (deciduous) teeth and will be replaced by adult ones. Provide larger chews and toys, as your puppy's jaw is getting stronger and needs an increasingly vigorous workout.

Check your puppy's weight regularly both at home and at the vet's, giving larger portions of food as he develops to keep his growth on track. The rate of weight gain will have slowed down in most smaller breed dogs by four months of age, while larger breed dogs continue to grow at a considerable rate.

Check your puppy's collar to ensure that it isn't too tight.

Travel requirements

If you have embarked on obtaining a pet passport, your puppy may need a blood test, which is due at least 30 days after his first rabies vaccination.

▼ Check your puppy's ears regularly and use a liquid cleaner if necessary to prevent infection.

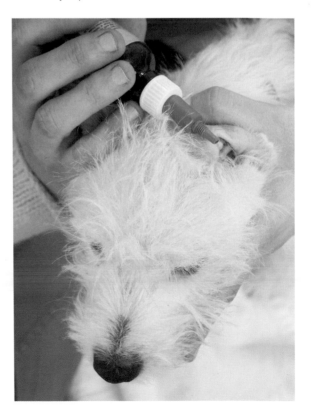

WEEKS 16–19: OWNER CHECKLISTS

What your puppy may do

- [ ] Misbehave in your presence and when left alone
- [ ] Bite the lead, bite others or bite you
- [ ] Resent being groomed or examined
- [ ] Be fearful of new things and even regress in confidence
- [ ] Have the occasional toileting accident indoors

What you should do

- [ ] Summon your patience to remain fair and consistent
- [ ] Don't allow your puppy to get away with bad behaviour
- [ ] Acclimatize him to being alone for up to three hours
- [ ] Keep him stimulated

Health reminders

- [ ] Worming and flea control are again needed
- [ ] Keep your puppy's nails in check by walking him on rough surfaces or trimming them
- [ ] Grooming procedures such as bathing, teeth cleaning and general checks should be routine
- [ ] Expect loss of teeth over the next few months

Weeks 20–24

Growing pains

This stage will see the relationship between you and your puppy move from parent and child towards mutual companionship. Growing pains that herald sexual maturity, akin to those of a human teenager, will test that happy picture. A higher level of training and specialist disciplines can now be explored, to mould him into the dog of your dreams.

PARENTAL DUTIES

Assess and adjust

Energetic, enthusiastic and bold, your much bigger puppy still has a great capacity to learn. Use this stage to take stock of your puppy's development and correct any deficiencies now. With improved experience and confidence on and off the lead, walking your puppy becomes less of a job and more of a joy.

YOUR PUPPY'S BEHAVIOUR

Look to his breeding

The breed of your puppy can again be used as an indicator of what behaviours to expect. A history of certain behavioural traits in the breed will encourage you to remain vigilant when setting him free within the confines of a 21st-century home and further afield.

Declaration of independence

Your puppy's newfound independence and free-thinking spirit will be appreciated when in the park, but may not be so welcome indoors, where mild destructiveness has become all-out war on your belongings. Chewing and tearing of fixtures and furnishings awaits owners of untrained, unexercised or unstimulated puppies. Trust to roam the whole home can only be given to the select few. Relaxation of confinement within your home can backfire for the over-eager owner, with housetraining taking a retrograde step and toileting accidents appearing in all manner of new places.

▲ Bolder, brighter and better behaved – the hopes for a puppy at this stage of development.

Big, bold and brash

Your puppy is a bigger, stronger and more self-aware animal at this stage, able to inflict serious injury if previous training has been lacking. Jumping up, biting and barging are all forms of rough play that he may attempt to indulge in, with a few ill-prepared owners now regretting obtaining their canine housemate. Some smaller breeds will be nearing their adult size, while larger breeds still have a way to go.

Puppy puberty

Smaller breeds will be moving into adolescence, so be prepared for the hormonal rollercoaster that this prequel to sexual maturity can bring. Scent marking and aggression, particularly towards other male dogs, can be seen in young males, while insecurity, indifference and mood swings greet the owners of female adolescent puppies. Female puppies can also regress in housetraining when they are in season, urinating and defecating indoors after months of not doing so.

These behaviours can wax and wane with either sex for a period of up to three years, as newly adult dogs come to terms with their surging hormone levels. Older puppies will have sexual desires and capabilities that must be curbed, as their physical development and maturity levels are insufficient to deal with the consequences.

WHAT YOUR PUPPY MAY DO

Behaviour that needs understanding

With the onset of sexual maturity, the behaviour of some male puppies can become generally unruly. Lifting his leg indoors to scent mark, becoming interested in female dogs or aggressive behaviour towards males, roaming and selective deafness when outdoors are all consistent with puppy growing pains. Female puppies during oestrus (heat) seem erratic and can become insecure, aggressive or subdued.

Behaviour that needs counteracting

With healthy growth and development, your maturing puppy can begin to overpower you with his exuberance and brute strength. If your pack leader status has not been properly confirmed,

▲ Insecurity, increased fearfulness or depression can be personality changes seen in female dogs on heat.

▶ Jumping up or aggressive behaviour may rear its head during this sometimes turbulent stage.

then confrontation leading to bites can take place. Aggressive tendencies around food may develop and major damage to household items as well as jumping onto furniture, visitors and you can all occur if your energetic and confident puppy has not been suitably parented. Mood swings and hormonal surges are negative influences that can lead to a lack of concentration and renewed house soiling, working against the positives of your puppy's renewed thirst for knowledge, game playing and training.

PAWS FOR THOUGHT
holding a grudge?

Like the question of whether dogs can feel guilt (see page 100), the ability of our canine comrades to hold a grudge is much debated by owners and scientists. Certainly dogs are able to remember an injustice dealt out by humans and other animals, being adept at avoiding confrontation and conflict. I have also heard many anecdotes of dogs holding subtle grudges, including one recently told to me by a friend.

A cross-bred, half-blind dog called Ratty is owned collectively by a surf company in the Algarve of Portugal, where I spent some time writing this book. One of my best mates, a surfing instructor called Sebastian, was driving a group of novice surfers out of town when he noticed that Ratty was in hot pursuit, as he was usually taken along on such trips. But during the summer months, dogs are forbidden from sharing the beach with holidaymakers, so Ratty had to be returned to town and left at the surf house. That evening, Sebastian attempted to make up for not taking Ratty to the beach by playing his favourite game of chasing an empty plastic bottle. Usually ecstatic about this game, Ratty snubbed Sebastian's attempts to cajole him, plodding off to sulk in the corner of the surf house.

Betty's behaviour has also prompted me to rethink the findings of academics on this matter, particularly her actions after being left at home for a series of short periods when I had three meetings over the course of one day. Although I walked her as much as normal, she found my final evening excursion to the gym one too many, depositing a huge bowel motion on the living room floor during my absence as if to say, 'Leave me again, eh? That'll teach you!' After not defecating in the house for over two months and being given adequate access outdoors to toilet during the day, what else is a rational owner to conclude?

WHAT YOU SHOULD DO

Dealing with sexual behaviours

Learning the signs of sexual maturity will help you to be prepared to deal with them when they inevitably arrive. Keep a close eye on your puppy's newfound interest in the opposite sex, which can

▲ Feed puppy last, so that he can fully appreciate that he sits at the bottom of the dominance hierarchy.

lead to unwanted pregnancy or aggression if it is allowed to go unchecked.

Day-to-day discipline

Continue to assert your pack leader status by eating first, passing through doors first and never accepting aggression. Consult an animal behaviourist if food aggression is experienced to avoid this worrying behaviour plaguing him (and you) into adulthood.

Exercise and training

Start exercising with your puppy more as he nears fully grown size, bearing in mind that he may have attained adult stature but has a way to go in the maturity stakes. Reconsider training classes if not already enrolled or look into specialized training and activities for your puppy to keep him stimulated.

◀ Agility training is an interesting way of challenging a maturing puppy.

BETTY'S DIARY
progress up to a point

Day 106 Pushing boundaries with your puppy can be fraught with failure. Modification of training regimes and freedoms granted depend on your puppy's varying responses. Betty was no different during this phase, giving me much to be proud of, while occasionally necessitating apologies.

With Betty changing from a black to a patchy wheat colour and nearing full size, her mental maturity still had some way to go. Well versed in basic training and toilet training at home, Betty was a joy and loved by all that met her. With much socialization and habituation as a younger puppy, she was completely at ease with traffic, other dogs and the varied residents of our friendly locality. She would routinely come when called in the park, after consistent use of long leads and treats when on our own, but could not be trusted completely off the lead when the park was shared by others. She could not resist meeting other dogs in her happy, confident way, which rarely elicited ill will, and meeting children brought a whole new meaning to the word 'excited'.

As previously mentioned, it is hard to train friends and family to be good dog trainers and verging on the impossible with children. Considering the speed with which Betty would rush to her child idols, it is understandable that this could result in fright. A jumping, flailing child is great entertainment for a perky puppy and Betty could never resist jumping up too – a scene I witnessed on Day 106. Thankfully, the parents of the frightened child were dog lovers and hoped their son would appreciate Betty's affections. I felt terrible that he had been upset even though Betty was completely friendly and just wanted to greet him. With time we coaxed a smile from the child and I held Betty safely so that she could gently lick his hand. After bidding the family farewell and walking home, I made a conscious decision to temper Betty's off-lead exploration while further improving her recall skills.

Lessons learned
Know your puppy, constantly assess your environment, modify your training plan if mistakes are made and have an apology ready if your puppy still manages to do the wrong thing.

▲ Bigger chews will give your puppy something to gnaw on and prevent mishaps.

HEALTH REMINDERS

Preventative treatments

The last of the monthly worming treatments is due, then treatments every three months are recommended. Flea-control application may be due again, depending on the product used.

Health checks and routines

Grooming and general health checks should be carried out on a regular basis. Adult teeth should be almost through, with a routine in place to keep them clean using daily teeth brushing and chews to ensure good dental health. Ear plucking may be required to keep your puppy's ear canals clear.

Toys and chews

Be on the lookout for great new toys that will stimulate your maturing puppy and help keep him out of mischief. Increase the size of chews and toys so that the potential for choking is minimized.

Neutering

As his hormones are racing, you should begin to consider the issue of neutering, which is generally carried out once your puppy has reached full maturity. Discuss the pros and cons with your vet.

▼ Keep your puppy stimulated as he grows by introducing him to new toys and environments.

PAWS FOR THOUGHT
guilty or not guilty?

Many behaviourists believe that guilt is an emotion only experienced by higher primates such as humans. But owners often report their canines acting guilty when they have perpetrated the unthinkable – for example, I have heard tales of owners finding an embarrassed-looking dog, then minutes later a chewed rug or steaming pile in the kitchen. Canine body language is subtle and complex, used to appease an unhappy superior member of the pack. This is also seen if something is found askew after leaving a puppy alone at home, your rising frustration and tension levels being easily detected by your attuned canine companion. They are much better natural readers of body language than us, so they may attempt to appease us with gestures that we incorrectly perceive as guilt.

Envy, guilt, spite and an ability to read their owners' minds are some of the complex skills that dog enthusiasts commonly claim to have found in their four-legged friends. What emotional complexities lie beneath the wheaten exterior of my Border Terrier's cranium? The jury is still out . . .

WEEKS 20–24: OWNER CHECKLISTS

What your puppy may do

- [ ] Overpower you with exuberance and brute strength
- [ ] Become increasingly destructive
- [ ] Show signs of sexual maturity
- [ ] Have a renewed thirst for knowledge, game playing and training

What you should do

- [ ] Deal with the signs of sexual maturity
- [ ] Check out advanced training classes
- [ ] Exercise your puppy more outdoors as he grows older and wiser
- [ ] Discuss behavioural concerns with professionals

Health reminders

- [ ] Baby teeth will continue to be lost as adult teeth come through; brushing should begin in earnest
- [ ] Monthly worming is again needed, plus flea treatments, depending on the preparation used
- [ ] Continue with regular grooming and health checks
- [ ] Monitor your puppy for changes associated with sexual maturity and consider neutering

6 months and beyond

The aspiring adult

Having matured under your watchful ownership, your young dog will continue to develop physically and emotionally over the next few years. Further training, attention, play and exercise will forge your relationship into one that will last a lifetime.

WHAT TO EXPECT
Size and weight
Smaller breeds will have reached their full-grown height and weight, while larger breed dogs continue growing until around 18 months to two years of age. The rate of weight gain for larger breed puppies will finally slow down from the massive gains of the last few months, already having markedly slowed in smaller breeds from around four months of age.

Behavioural and social development
Behaviour will vary greatly in your puppy depending on breed and the degree of training, socialization and habituation that he has received, with lessons continuing to be learned into adulthood. Sexual maturity will bring with it additional behavioural challenges. Using strong and confident leadership with kindness, patience and understanding, owners can help to alleviate and overcome these usually transient issues.

YOUR PUPPY'S BEHAVIOUR
Energy driven
Whether your young dog is tenacious or rebellious, exuberant or over-excited, it is how you channel his energy that changes the way you perceive it. Begin to venture more deeply into the world of experiences and challenges that you can share with your dog, gradually increasing the difficulty of training. Also extend outdoor activities on a social level, allowing interactions with many other non-threatening dogs and humans.

Sexual maturity
Sexual behaviours will begin to surface at this stage of development, and can be addressed with patience, vigilance or neutering. Hormone surges can lead to some erratic behaviour, with certain individuals challenging humans in a bid to assert dominance further.

Fear revisited
Fearful tendencies can again be exhibited at this adolescent stage, commonly reported in young

▲ Be patient with your six-month-old puppy. He may be nearing his mature size but he still has lots to learn.

male dogs. Owner frustration and impatience at this sudden shyness are understandable, but comforting your puppy and thereby affirming his fears is an unhelpful response and a common mistake. Fear aggression can be exhibited, and protectiveness of belongings or you may be new concerns to deal with.

Challenges ahead
Be mindful that your dog may be approaching his adult size, but has much to learn and experience before he reaches emotional maturity. Be realistic with your expectations, appreciating that one foolish overestimation of your puppy's maturity and experience level can lead to emotional scars that may never heal. With a full set of adult teeth, it can be disappointing to see a reoccurrence of chewing – a phase of territorial exploration that tends to pass quickly.

WHAT YOUR PUPPY MAY DO
Physical changes

Your small breed puppy may reach full height, while continuing to gain weight until one year. If a larger breed puppy, he is likely to continue to grow in height and weight up until two years of age. His fur may also change, with his soft puppy coat being slowly replaced by a generally thicker adult coat.

In the case of a poorly considered or unlucky puppy purchase, your growing dog may begin to exhibit signs of congenital (from birth) medical diseases as he reaches adult size.

Behavioural changes

Your six-month-old dog may be newly fearful or shy of familiar objects and people. This is just something that can occur in puppies of this age, although most will be happily enjoying life in general. With sexual maturity, he may attempt to move up the dominance rankings in your pack. This needs to be quelled quickly. Showing new territorial or protective traits around the home and family, your young dog may dislike or display aggression towards other dogs of the same sex.

WHAT YOU SHOULD DO
Exercise and training

Focus on increased complexity of training and exposure to new environments, negotiated by you to avoid fear-evoking situations. Take a step back to assess your dog's progress, training yourself not to confront or comfort him when nervous or fearful. That said, remind yourself that you are the owner of a big puppy not a fully grown dog, and check out new ways to interact with him if he is inherently nervous in order to build his confidence.

Dealing with sexual behaviours

Remember that sexual maturity brings hormonally charged behavioural changes within your older puppy, particularly towards other dogs. Do your utmost to assess other dogs at a distance before

◀ He may be an adult but don't ask for trouble – pick up anything you don't want chewed.

allowing your dog to interact with them. If you have concerns regarding your dog's developing sexuality, discuss them with your vet while investigating the possibility of neutering.

Day-to-day discipline

Continue to be a strong and confident leader without relaxing established codes of behaviour. Halt any rough play that can further stimulate your maturing dog to challenge you and assert his dominance. Finally, congratulate yourself on raising your puppy into a healthy dog and look forward to a rewarding and happy life together.

When to neuter

Canines should be allowed to gain full physical maturity prior to neutering, which is best gauged by sexual development. It is advisable to neuter female dogs after their first season, waiting at least a month after signs of bleeding before booking them in for the procedure. This allows for reproductive organs to reduce in size and blood-carrying capacity, making the procedure safer to perform with fewer complications. The standard minimum age for neutering dogs is six to nine months.

OLD WIVES' TAIL

A bitch should have one litter of puppies before she is spayed, as it is important for her to become fully developed.

No, this is not the case. If every owner of a female dog thought that, the world would be over-run with unwanted puppies! Spaying helps to keep unplanned pregnancies to a minimum, while decreasing the chances of your dog suffering mammary tumours later in life. Uterine infections and ovarian cancer are no longer a concern once your bitch is neutered, nor will she continue to go through the behavioural highs and lows associated with seasons. If your female dog doesn't have puppies, she will be the same dog as if she had had them, without the potential health risks.

▼ Carry on exposing your puppy to different sights and sounds by taking him on lots of interesting walks.

JUDGING MATURITY

Differences between the breeds

Each breed matures differently, with the average dog reaching adult height at around nine months of age. Weight is determined by breed, diet and exercise, with a healthy larger dog continuing to gain muscle bulk until around 18 months of age. Adolescence is usually gauged by sexual maturity, which manifests itself in each sex differently. In females it is the physical development of oestrus (heat), that is, when they come into season. Males change more behaviourally, with scent marking and aggression towards other male dogs commonly seen.

Female sexual characteristics
- Swelling of vulva
- Bloody discharge for 5–7 days
- Mood swings from overly affectionate to insecure, aggressive or subdued
- Hiding toys
- Apparent withdrawal from the pack or the family
- Increase or decrease in appetite
- Develops pica (appetite for strange foods, such as rocks, earth, etc.)

Male sexual characteristics
- Lifts leg to urinate, scent marking numerous trees and vertical objects in neighbourhood and occasionally in house
- Challenges owners
- Dislikes or fights other male dogs
- Overly excitable
- Shows attraction to female dogs
- Imitates sexual acts with furniture, stuffed toys, young children or legs of adults
- Exhibits sexual arousal
- Generally unruly
- Roams
- Fails to be attentive when outdoors
- Lack of appetite

▼ Boys will be boys – sexual maturity can make your male dog a handful when you take him outdoors.

THE BREED GROUPS AT SIX MONTHS OLD

▲ A Scottish Terrier (terrier dog) is usually near full height, but will get slightly stockier with time.

▲ A Chihuahua (toy dog) is fully grown at six months and usually at or near full weight.

▶ At six months, a Border Collie (pastoral dog) still has some growing to do. It will achieve its full height within a few months.

▼ A St Bernard (working dog) can continue to grow in height and weight until 18–24 months.

▼ An Akita (utility dog) will continue to grow in height until around 12 months and fill out in weight until 18 months.

HEALTH REMINDERS

Preventative treatments

Worming treatments are now given every three months. Flea treatment can be used consistently or during the warmer months in non-allergic dogs. Other parasitic treatments may be necessary depending on where you live. Familiarize yourself with local disease-carrying parasites and purchase preventatives to combat them.

▼ Examine your dog closely when you stroke him to catch any minor problems early.

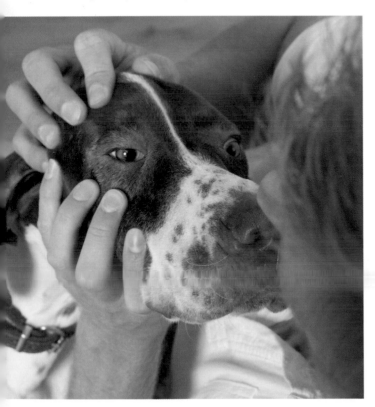

▲ Consult your vet about treatments that will combat any parasites that might be picked up in the park.

Health checks and routines

Plan yearly visits to your vet for general health check-ups, when one-off booster vaccinations of the standard vaccinations administered in the early stages of puppyhood are usually given.

Routinely examine your dog when stroking him, so that any changes in his condition or concerns about his health can be quickly addressed. Make sure you understand the signs of illness that a canine may exhibit (see page 137) so that your dog gets veterinary attention at an early stage when he needs it most.

Grooming may need to be more regular during coat change to deal with increased hair loss. You should continue to keep dental hygiene a priority with daily teeth brushing or dental chews.

Feeding

Re-assess your dog's nutritional requirements in consultation with your vet, checking to see if he is ready to graduate from puppy to adult foods.

Neutering

Neutering is normally recommended at the stage when your dog is fully grown in height and weight (see page 110).

First aid

Find time to familiarize yourself with canine first-aid techniques so that you can aid your dog if he injures himself or other emergency situations occur where his wellbeing is under threat (see page 143).

BETTY'S DIARY
from puppy to dog

Days 135–138 With the tell-tale signs of swollen vulva and reclusive behaviour, Betty became an adult by coming into season. Slightly off-colour for a day or two, she had a very small amount of bloody discharge and hid her toys under the sofa. Disappointingly, she suddenly began to urinate in the house again. Examination by her veterinarian father revealed a urine infection that required treatment. After a few days the worse of the (still minimal) bleeding had resolved and toileting accidents in the house also improved with a course of antibiotics.

In terms of her behaviour, Betty suddenly graduated from occasional puppy misdemeanours to a more mature, lady-like attitude, obeying house rules and following commands when outdoors with greater understanding and conviction. She was given a freer reign in her indoor pursuits as a reward for her newfound appreciation of living in a human world, which included asking to go outside to the toilet, eating well at allotted feeding times and relinquishment of her love of chewing remote controls, all of which were warmly welcomed. Result!

Lessons learned

Behavioural changes in your maturing puppy may be subtle and can indicate the onset of adulthood or illness, or both! Continue to challenge your developing puppy with greater freedoms indoors and extension of socialization and experience outdoors. Appreciate how much patience has gone into getting your puppy to this stage and pat yourself on the back for a job well done.

NEUTERING

What it involves
Neutering is the surgical removal of the organs involved in reproduction – the testicles in males or the ovaries and uterus of females. This is the most common procedure performed by vets on pet dogs. It is a routine operation carried out under general anaesthetic.

The arguments for and against
Historically, neutering has been used to decrease unwanted pregnancy in females and control male aggression or dominance. Many recent studies have proven a distinct health advantage in neutering canines of both sexes at a young age, with a decrease in the incidence of malignant tumour development later in life. Some male owners feel that castrating a male dog is taking away his life force, yet a pet dog lives his whole life sexually frustrated in forced celibacy. Female dogs are prone to uterine infections (pyometra) later in life, which are prevented with the removal of the uterus if spayed as a youngster.

Many owners wish to have one litter of puppies prior to having their bitch spayed, yet aren't fully aware of the potential complications that can await their beloved female canine, such as the death of puppies, still-born puppies, death of the mother, post-parturition uterine infections or poor mothering leading to the owner needing to feed the puppies every 3 to 4 hours with supplementary food. Puppies can be a real joy when they are healthy and well looked after by their canine mum, but be mindful that your puppies may be purchased at the expense of others in the community that desperately need homes.

Your dog is prone to weight gain post neutering, but strict monitoring of exercise and nutrition can avoid this potential side effect. I recommend neutering for all animals that will not be used for breeding, those suffering congenital disease or exhibiting hormonal-related behavioural problems. Every pet of mine has been neutered in the past without complication. There are strong arguments and emotive views on both sides to neuter or not to neuter, so it comes down to personal choice, along with your dog's individuality firmly in mind. This decision should only be made after thorough consultation with your vet.

Pros of neutering males
- Decrease in aggressive tendencies
- Decrease in crazed behaviour when a local bitch is in season
- Controls hypersexuality
- Reduction in prevalence of prostatic disease and cancer
- Eliminates risk of testicular cancer
- Helps to resolve unwanted 'mounting' behaviour
- Becomes calmer and more obedient

Pros of neutering females
- Avoids unwanted puppies
- Decrease in risk of mammary tumours
- Decrease in risk of sexually transmitted disease
- Eliminates risk of ovarian cancer and uterine infections (pyometra)
- Eliminates seasons/bleeding
- Avoids the mood swings that tend to occur with hormonal surges

Cons of neutering
- Unable to parent puppies
- Can lose instinct needed for hunting
- Risk of general anaesthetic and post-op complications
- Risk of weight gain
- A few females can develop hormonal-related incontinence later in life
- Behavioural changes may not suit certain canine professions, such as guard dogs

6 MONTHS PLUS: OWNER CHECKLISTS

What your puppy may do

- [ ] Reach full height, continuing to fill out until up to two years of age
- [ ] Show signs of sexual maturity and behaviour
- [ ] Be newly fearful or shy of familiar objects and people
- [ ] Become increasingly dominant, territorial or protective
- [ ] Dislike or show outward aggression towards other dogs of the same sex

What you should do

- [ ] Increase training and exposure to new environments, while avoiding fear-evoking situations
- [ ] Continue to be a strong and confident leader without relaxing established codes of behaviour
- [ ] Check out new ways to interact with your young dog to build his confidence
- [ ] Congratulate yourself on raising your puppy and look forward to enjoying life together

Health reminders

- [ ] Worm your dog every three months and apply anti-parasitic medications as recommended by your vet
- [ ] Consider neutering
- [ ] Reassess your dog's diet
- [ ] Plan to bring your dog to the vet at least once a year for a general health check-up
- [ ] Groom and examine your dog regularly to pick up early warning signs of disease and maintain dental hygiene with teeth brushing or dental chews
- [ ] Familiarize yourself with canine first aid, as well as the signs of illness in dogs

To find out more on . . .

Aggression and biting, go to page 113
Basic training exercises, go to page 68
Common puppy illnesses, go to page 138
Chewing, go to page 124
Flea control, go to page 42
Grooming, go to page 60
Mounting, go to page 121
Puppy first aid, go to page 143
Puppy training classes, go to page 82
Nervousness and fear, go to page 130
Socialization and habituation, go to page 55
Tick, lice and mite control, go to page 42
Vaccinations, go to page 39
Worming, go to page 40

Problem solver
Coping with bad behaviour

Puppies can be expected to exhibit all manner of behaviours, some of which their owners will find undesirable. Understanding why these unwanted behaviours occur can help to prevent them becoming a lifelong problem and addressing the early warning signs immediately will avoid the need to implement cures in the future.

Aggression and biting

A degree of **biting** and **mock-aggressive** playful behaviour is to be expected in a young, confident puppy finding his feet and very rarely will he bite to cause actual harm. But biting or aggression in adult dogs can have **serious ramifications** for both you and your dog, so must be dealt with swiftly in your puppy through **training and socialization.**

WHY

Play

Biting and mouthing his littermates is the only play behaviour your puppy knows before arriving at your home. When interacting with you he may continue this behaviour, mouthing your hands and feet in the same way he did his siblings to initiate a game. This behaviour is particularly undesirable when delicate-skinned children or the elderly are present, especially considering how sharp a young puppy's teeth can be. If allowed to continue, this type of playful biting can lead to injury and occasionally the development of aggressive tendencies in extreme cases. Chasing feet or clothing as you walk past is great fun and can also stimulate a puppy to play bite. This inappropriate behaviour must also be quickly quelled to avoid injury or damage.

Fear

This is the most common reason for a puppy to bite strangers. A puppy will rarely bite out of fear when he is young, preferring to hide behind his owner or rapidly remove himself from a frightening situation. But, as he grows older and more confident, your puppy may start to use biting to defend himself in situations from which he cannot escape. Once a puppy begins biting, he can realize how effectively it can be used to get out of an unpleasant experience and he may begin using it as a first line of defence towards other dogs and strange people.

Dominance/status-related aggression

Some puppies will vie for leadership of the pack, biting their owners or family members during play or confrontation in an attempt to command the situation. A naturally more confident puppy will resort to aggression towards others more readily than a shy individual if he feels threatened. Appreciating that your puppy is a more dominant animal early on and responding accordingly is important to avoid aggression issues as he grows.

Miscommunication

Dogs have many ways of showing that they are angry or fearful without resorting to biting. Vocalizations such as barking or growling and body language such as pinned-back ears, bared teeth and erect fur are used by dogs to avoid conflict. Many new owners are not well versed in canine body language and an inexperienced puppy may not be sufficiently familiar with the body language displayed by other dogs, so any actual physical aggression that takes place can often be blamed on miscommunication.

Resource/food-related aggression

Some puppies will feel the need to guard their food and this can become a serious issue, especially when there are young children residing in the same household. This sort of aggression is seen more commonly in puppies that have suffered from lack of food in the past. It can be considered a reversion to wild dog behaviour, when individuals needed to protect the food they had acquired from others in the pack.

PREVENTION

Predictability

Learn the basics of canine body language (see page 50), as being able to read adeptly the signs that your puppy uses to communicate his feelings will avoid aggressive tendencies becoming the norm. At an early age, your puppy will only bite when playing, so always have toys at the ready to substitute for your hand.

If your puppy is a keen biter of skirts, trouser legs or feet as they swish past, keep him secure in a play pen in a high-traffic area of your home so that he gets used to them without being able to react. When your puppy begins going outside, he may be fearful of other dogs and people. Never force an interaction or meeting that may stimulate fear, protecting your puppy at all times from frightening situations to avoid aggression.

Socialization and habituation

Ensuring that your puppy is well socialized with other people and dogs (once he has been fully vaccinated), and exposing him to many potentially frightening places and objects in a calm and relaxed way is the best technique to avoid fear-related aggression (see page 55). Be careful to avoid reinforcement of fear through comforting your puppy, allowing him instead to shrug off initial fears before gaining his confidence.

Avoiding force

It is important always to bear in mind that treating aggression with aggression simply will not work. If anything, shouting or using force will escalate the situation further or result in your puppy learning to use aggression more readily next time. Remember that fear is at the root of most of the aggressive behaviours in your puppy, so you should try to avoid physical punishment at all costs and instead search for a considered solution. Any verbal punishment that you apply should only be loud enough to halt the misdemeanour, without instilling fear in your puppy.

Training

A well-trained dog is a well-adjusted dog that will respond to your every command (see page 68). Once you have identified a potentially dangerous situation, it means that you will be able to extricate your puppy from harm before any aggression manifests itself.

CURE

Play with toys

By using appropriate substitutes for arms and clothing in play biting, your puppy will eventually learn what is acceptable to bite and what isn't. Shake toys to stimulate play or use toys that squeak to keep your puppy's interest on the toy and not on your hand. Be patient, as biting is a lesson that needs to be unlearned from your puppy's time with his siblings, and playing with toys initially seems far less fun to him than playing rough games with you.

Tell him it hurts

If your puppy is consistently biting you during play, loudly say 'ouch' while standing up and ignoring him. This will momentarily halt his biting, teaching him that aggression towards you will result in the end of play. If he leans towards you with his mouth open during play, quietly command 'no' and reward him with affection if he stops. Even if a biting incident is deemed accidental, you should halt the game immediately so that he quickly learns that teeth are not allowed.

▶ Play with toys not your hands, teaching your puppy what is acceptable for him to bite and what isn't.

Time out

Keeping a collar on your puppy and a lead in your pocket at all times indoors is handy for separating a puppy from excitable children or leading him into another room as a form of non-confrontational punishment. If a play session results in your puppy biting you, say 'no', then lead him into another room to calm the situation down for a few minutes – the puppy should then make the connection between biting/aggression and being separated from the pack. Children playing inappropriately with your puppy can cause this potentially dangerous behaviour to continue for longer. Teach them how to play with him using toys to keep activity sessions positive and safe (see page 25).

▼ If over-excitement leads to bites, impose a time-out to teach your puppy that aggression is not acceptable.

▲ You can overcome guarding behaviour by training your puppy to allow you to lift the food bowl mid-meal.

Reward positive behaviour

Train your puppy to overcome his fears by rewarding calm behaviour. When a previously feared stimulus such as another dog or stranger is at a safe distance to avoid provoking a fearful response, reward your puppy for being relaxed by initiating a game or feeding him a treat. Repeat the process with patience and caution, bringing either your puppy closer to the stimulus or vice versa until he is acting calmly without initiating any aggression.

Symbolic gestures

Making some basic changes to routine, such as feeding your dog last and not allowing him to walk ahead of you through doors, is an effective means

of teaching your puppy about his low rank in your pack. His perceived status should fall below yours and your family in the pecking order – a subordinate animal is much less likely to bite a more dominant one. Involve all family members in feeding and training so that the puppy realizes that he needs to perform certain actions for all family members to be rewarded.

Give and take

A puppy who guards his food bowl from you believes that you are going to take his food away. Firstly, train all family members never to take food or treats away from your puppy if he growls when they approach and to avoid escalating any aggression by shouting at him. Train your puppy to welcome your approach towards his food bowl by bringing him something even more tasty than he is already consuming. Once he is ready to allow your approach, begin to lift the bowl out of his reach mid-meal, placing a few treats in his bowl before replacing it. In the case where he has hold of something potentially dangerous, the minimum amount of force should be used to remove the offending item and you should offer a more attractive alternative to end the situation positively.

Animal behaviourists

Animal behaviourists delve into the cause, function, development and evolution of behaviour in animals and relate this knowledge to the treatment of behavioural problems in pets and wild animals. Given that behavioural issues in companion animals are quite complex, qualified behaviourists and counsellors are recommended by veterinarians to help distraught owners deal with their problem pets.

Consulting an animal behaviourist is advisable if your puppy seems to be developing worrying behaviours, such as biting, which you are unable to halt or control. Your vet will only be able to advise you so far, because, without seeing how you interact with your puppy on

walks and in your home environment, he or she won't have access to all the information needed to solve the problem. An animal behaviourist will visit your home, observe your puppy, discuss the issue at length and devise appropriate and practical solutions.

Always gain the services of a specialist animal behaviourist through your veterinarian by referral, as this will enable you to locate the most experienced and qualified practitioners in your area to help solve your puppy's problem.

Over-excitement

Every dog owner wants their puppy to **greet** visitors enthusiastically and **without fear**. As many visitors will also be pleased to meet him, the combination can result in a puppy that **constantly jumps up** when meeting **new people** or in exciting situations. Endearing in a small puppy, this behaviour can become a **real nuisance** in an older, **heavier dog**, leading to complaints about **muddy paw prints** and even **injury**.

WHY

Canine greetings

Face-to-face greetings are a natural way for two dogs to meet. As we are bipedal (stand on two legs), your face is much removed from your puppy, resulting in him wanting to get closer to it by jumping up to say hello.

Attention seeking

A puppy will quickly learn that jumping up at people gains a response, either positive or negative. In the early days, your puppy will cause little damage or injury indoors, so the behaviour cycle of jumping up followed by attention is allowed to continue.

Bad table manners

As dogs are natural scavengers, your puppy will quickly appreciate that when you or your family sit down to the table, tasty titbits will follow. He will learn that these morsels come from the table and may begin to jump up to get closer to the food supply in order to help himself.

Untrained others

As a general rule, this behaviour is not performed with members of the family who are well versed in dog training. However, other people whom the puppy meets will often allow him to jump up, making it very difficult to reinforce the lesson that it is not an acceptable way for him to behave. Also, many people are not dog lovers and they may find it off-putting if your puppy jumps up to greet them.

◀ Canines naturally meet face-to-face and this is a reason why your dog will jump up to say hello.

▲ One way of preventing your puppy from jumping up is to get down to his level to meet him.

PREVENTION

Greet him at his level

Crouch down to his level immediately on your arrival home or whenever you are giving him attention, so that you don't encourage jumping up in the first place. Teach visitors to react similarly when your puppy approaches them.

Restrain him

Use a lead on your puppy both indoors and out or hold him when he is meeting people, especially children, so that he does not automatically jump up at them as his standard greeting.

No table treating

Teach all the family and your friends not to treat the dog when they are sitting at the dining table so that he doesn't expect to get any food treats when you sit down to eat.

Basic training

Training your puppy to return to you as soon as he is called (see page 68) will help to prevent him from making contact with fellow park goers who are not so keen on dogs or who are unaware how to interact with an excitable puppy. Once he is securely on his lead, you can decide whether the interaction is a good idea or not. When allowing him to meet people, use the lead or a hand on his collar to prevent him jumping up.

CURE

Ignorance is bliss

Make it a rule not to give your puppy any attention until all four feet are on the ground. Boredom is a powerful tool to use in disciplining your puppy. By ignoring him, he will quickly lose interest in you, stop jumping up and walk off. As soon as he calms down, command him to come to you and sit, then crouch down to give him the attention he deserves for good behaviour. It is almost impossible to use this technique when your large breed puppy grows and still jumps up, so use it while you still can.

Teach others how to react

Giving visitors to your home a quick lesson in how to react when your puppy jumps up is paramount in training him not to do so. Children in particular need guidance, as their excitable natures tend to incite your puppy to jump up at them. Teach visitors to stand up straight, with arms folded and looking away from the puppy. Tell them to use the command 'no' calmly when the puppy jumps up, then command him to 'sit'.

When the correct behaviours are performed, visitors should immediately crouch down to give the puppy praise and treats. If the puppy again lunges playfully for the face, tell them to retreat and halt all contact until he is again still. Consider recruiting understanding friends and family for the training process, repeating the exercise as many times as possible.

Avoid physical or verbal punishment

Pushing your puppy away or verbally reprimanding him harshly can be interpreted by your puppy as an encouragement to play rough in the same way. This may worsen the situation, occasionally leading to a further escalation of playful or aggressive responses in your maturing puppy (see page 89). Just one firm 'no', followed by ignoring, should discourage your puppy from jumping up.

◀ Ask visitors to ignore your puppy until he is calm and has all four paws on the ground.

Mounting

An **extension of jumping up** that has **sexual overtones**, mounting can be regarded by owners as anything from horrifying to amusing. Trying to mount another puppy or a person is fairly **normal canine behaviour** that in most cases is **not sexual** in nature. The behaviour is observable in **male and female** puppies from a few months of age into **sexual maturity** and beyond.

WHY

Play

In young puppies, mounting tends to be a playful behaviour between individuals, when they jump on top of each other and roll around in half-hearted fighting. Excessive play with owners or the arrival of visitors can stimulate this behaviour, which your puppy enacts to release anxiety and tension.

Dominance display

In wild dogs, mounting a member of the pack is a clear statement of dominance and higher ranking. This ranking gives rights to females and other resources coveted by the pack. In domestic dogs, a puppy may constantly mount as a sign of insecurity, in an attempt to assert his dominance over family members.

Sexual contact

During puberty, a male dog can be seen to mount other dogs and people in response to surging testosterone levels.

PREVENTION

Remind him who is top dog

From the earliest opportunity, make it clear that you are the alpha dog in your pack and that family members all rank above your new puppy. He will be a much calmer and happier dog knowing his position in the world than one constantly, and in this case inappropriately, fighting for supremacy.

CURE

Increase exercise intensity

Burn off your puppy's excess energy, which can lead to mounting, by exercising him more vigorously.

Keep him calm

Remove him from living areas until visitors have sat down, then keep his attention with treats.

Don't shake your leg

This will heighten the reward gained by a mounting puppy. Advise visitors to keep their leg still while detaching the puppy without giving him undue attention. Call him away and reward him for doing so.

Neutering

If you think the mounting is sexual or occurs as your puppy reaches puberty, ask your vet about neutering (see page 110). Around one-third of castrated males show immediate improvement due to decreased testosterone. Female dogs seen mounting during heat have also improved after being spayed.

Do nothing

With consistent training and exercise, your puppy will hopefully grow out of this behaviour in time.

Excessive vocalization

Barking is a **normal vocalization** made by dogs (except of course the barkless Basenji) to **communicate** with each other and guard their environment. After aggression, **excessive vocalization** is the next most likely cause of **complaint** to be levelled at your dog and you. A problem regularly facing the owners of fast-reacting, edgy canines such as **terriers**, this nuisance behaviour is more common in **smaller breed** dogs.

WHY

Attention seeking

This is the most common cause of excessive barking in your young puppy. After leaving the comfort of mum and siblings, vocalization is one way your puppy can learn to get your attention when he wants it. This is not a natural behaviour for a young canine, as in the wild it would be likely to draw unwanted attention from predators.

Guarding territory

One of the reasons that dogs were first invited into human homes was as a guard, warning their owners of an intruder with successive barks. This trait was then selectively bred to improve their guarding abilities, resulting in certain breeds being particularly vocal.

Boredom or frustration

Being bored or left on their own can trigger a dog to bark in an attempt to be reunited with other members of his pack (you and your family). This may begin as occasional barking, but can graduate to bouts of howling.

Fear or anxiety

Any perceived threat may stimulate your puppy to bark as a way to ward off danger or alert the rest of the pack. Usually reserved for unfamiliar people or objects, these high-pitched barks tend to make your puppy feel better, thus encouraging him to continue barking.

PREVENTION

Ignorance is bliss

You *must* ignore your puppy when he is barking for attention, otherwise he will quickly learn that you will come whenever he calls. As you would ignore a child throwing a tantrum, only give attention to your puppy when he is quiet and well behaved. If he tries to gain freedom from a play pen by whining or barking, talk soothingly and don't look at him. Only pay him direct attention when he is silent.

Don't encourage him

A barking young puppy can be very cute, but giving him attention for it is a recipe for disaster. Never encourage him to bark, as this will be the first method chosen to express himself as he matures, resulting in an overly vocal dog.

Socialization

The more socialized a puppy is, the less he fears, which means the less he feels the need to bark. Avoiding potentially frightening situations also helps to avoid excessive vocalization becoming the norm.

COMMON QUESTIONS
barking

My puppy is driving me crazy with his incessant barking. I have tried everything to stop him. Should I use one of those shock barking collars as a last resort?

Do *not* use collars that give your puppy an electric shock each time they bark – these are cruel and don't address the cause of barking in the first place. If barking is a major concern, seek the professional advice of an animal behaviourist (see page 117), who will be able to help you tackle the problem without resorting to physical torture.

Stimulation

Provide lots of toys and treats throughout the day at varying times so that your puppy never feels neglected or bored. Training is a good opportunity to allow your dog to communicate with you in non-verbal ways.

CURE
Reward quietness

Rewarding your puppy when he is silent around previously bark-stimulating or frightening things is a difficult technique to master, as it requires attentiveness and quick thinking. Barking can be quite tiring for your puppy and using this approach will soon teach him that being quiet is a much more successful and less labour-intensive strategy.

Territorial modification

If your puppy is the guarding type, block his access to stimuli that cause him to bark. Don't allow him to have direct access to the front door where visitors and mail may arrive and put him away briefly when visitors come to the door. If you notice territorial barking, common to fast-reacting edgy breeds such as terriers, block his view through your front windows to avoid excessive vocalization aimed at passers-by.

▼ Toys will keep your puppy entertained – and chewing on them also makes it difficult to bark!

Chewing

Chewing is a **normal** and **natural** behaviour and should be expected throughout your puppy's life, even well into adulthood. Gaining a good **understanding** of chewing while your puppy is young should help you **avoid home devastation** when he gets older . . . and stronger!

WHY

Wild tendencies

After wild dogs have caught and killed their prey, they are faced with the hard task of devouring it. This requires patient chewing of the carcass, tearing at the skin, bone and sinew. Your puppy will exhibit this genetically inherited behaviour when chewing in your home, for instance when he holds a ball down and attempts to tear off its exterior, in the same way that a wild dog would deal with captured prey in the wild.

Breed

Some specific breeds of dog, such as gundogs, have been trained for many years to fetch hunted game. Using their mouths from an early age is therefore an integral part of their growth and learning process.

Teething

In the same way as human babies, puppies go through a teething process. In dogs this usually occurs from three to six months of age, with most breeds having adult teeth by six to seven months. Chewing can help to alleviate some of the discomfort of teething, encourage the baby (deciduous) teeth to fall out and stimulate the growth of adult teeth.

Exploration

Because they have a high concentration of nerve receptors along the gumline, puppies benefit from exploring different aspects of objects through chewing, such as texture and consistency. Investigation of their environment in this way can continue until adulthood, which, in large breed dogs, extends to around 18 months of age.

PREVENTION

Vigilance

There's a simple rule when your puppy is very young: don't trust him! You should puppy proof your home thoroughly by keeping all chewable or valuable items off the floor, lifting electrical wires out of reach and putting shoes in cupboards (see page 32). Consider buying a play pen when you can't constantly watch your puppy to keep him enclosed in a safe area, filled only with his own things (see page 58).

Toys

These should be carefully chosen to have a different texture to everyday objects in the home. Rubber toys are ideal, as a dog cannot mistake them for cloth or wood. These toys can be made more appealing by placing flavoured pastes or treats inside them, which will keep your puppy entertained for hours. Always remember to check toys and replace them if they become damaged, as parts can dislodge and could injure your puppy or be swallowed by him.

Chews

Both rawhide and commercially-made chews will give your puppy the opportunity to satiate his need to chew on a tasty morsel, while cleaning his teeth and stimulating his gums at the same time. Only give your puppy chews when you are around, so that you are on hand in case he has any difficulties. You should also be sure to use them sparingly, as many chews are high in fat and can lead to dogs developing weight problems.

CURE
Caught in the act

Don't verbally reprimand a puppy when you catch him in the act of chewing, as you will make him wary of you and this may lead to your puppy targeting the same object but out of your sight. It is best that your puppy feels confident enough to chew in front of you so that you are able to control what he has access to and avoid destruction of precious belongings. Taking care to prevent him seeing that it comes from you, use a water spray to spray your puppy when he chews something he shouldn't. When he stops, start up a game with appropriate chew toys, rewarding him with praise at the same time.

BETTY'S DIARY
list of carnage

During the first six months of her life, Betty managed to chew her way through the following off-limits items:

- 1 wallet full of cash and credit cards
- 1 pair of swimming goggles
- 1 standing wooden mask
- numerous odd socks, which later reappeared with large holes
- 2 remote controls
- 1 personal cheque
- selection of garden plants
- 2 telephone directories
- 1 work shoe
- 1 shirt off the clothes line (hours before I needed it to go on television!)
- loads of bark removed from the garden and strewn around the house
- 2 DVDs

Lessons learned

If you don't want any household or personal item chewed, keep it out of reach of your puppy and provide suitable chewable alternatives. Looking on the positive side, I have never kept my home so tidy!

Deterrents

Effective deterrents in the form of bitter sprays are readily available from pet stores. These sprays are a harmless way of protecting larger items from your puppy's over-active jaws. Spraying is a particularly good strategy for objects that can't be hidden away from your puppy, such as table legs or sofa cushions. However, the sprays may stain so make sure you test them first on a small area of the object to be treated.

Mix it up

Change the range of toys and chews available to your puppy so that boredom doesn't set in and lead him astray. You can build up a stock of toys with different shapes and consistencies and rotate them on a weekly basis.

Don't give in

Just because your puppy has destroyed an off-limits object doesn't mean that you should then allow him to have the ruined item as a chew plaything, for example a pair of chewed-up shoes. This will confuse him, as there will be no clear boundary between what he is allowed to chew and what he isn't. Take destroyed articles away calmly and encourage your puppy to play only with his own toys. Don't become complacent as your puppy grows, because with age come stronger jaws and an ability to cause greater damage.

Environmental correction

In this training approach, you make it appear to the puppy that the environment reacts negatively to bad behaviour. Best-known examples are using a water pistol or banging pans together whenever your puppy is about to behave inappropriately. He will assume that the negative reaction has come from whatever he is interested in and will move away to find something else to investigate.

Most puppies realize that they can take liberties when you are not home, as there will be little to stop them jumping up onto work surfaces to steal food or raiding the rubbish bin. A puppy will continue to perform a bad behaviour for as long as it feels good, therefore as an owner you need to manipulate his environment so that being mischievous when you are not around can be frightening and far from rewarding.

This can be done by setting harmless booby traps for a misbehaving home-alone puppy, which may only need to be set once for your puppy not to re-offend. Leaving a shirt with a long sleeve dangling over the side of a counter may give a bored puppy the perfect excuse to pull it off for a good chew. By placing a number of cans filled with buttons over the shirt, you will give your puppy just enough fright when they clatter to the floor that he will not consider doing it again. Another example would be to apply a bitter spray around the rim of your empty rubbish bin, with just the tiniest taste repelling your puppy for life.

Environmental corrections should always be discussed with a vet, dog trainer or animal behaviourist first to determine the right amount of fright to give your puppy without causing long-lasting anxiety.

House soiling

Urinating and defecating in the home despite all efforts to housetrain is a common reason for frustrated owners to consider re-homing their puppy. Remember that your puppy is likely to continue making the occasional toileting mistake up to six months of age and beyond, and recognize that certain factors out of his control such as ill health or a change of routine can lead to a backward training step.

WHY

Lack of patience

Owners often do not show enough patience with their young charges when it comes to toilet training, resulting in a puppy that is frightened to toilet anywhere near their owner and 'accidents' that are found out of sight all over the home.

Incomplete toilet training

When a puppy finally takes himself outdoors to urinate, owners are frequently so overwhelmed with relief that they stop actively toilet training forthwith. Others will keep a dog kennelled outdoors or left in the garden for an hour or two without giving appropriate instruction or reward for going in the right place. This can result in a dog that, if unable to go outside, will go indoors without concern.

Delayed punishment

Scolding your puppy for going to the toilet indoors after the event is pointless and can potentially make the situation worse. Your puppy will not be able to relate the verbal punishment with the earlier misdemeanour of going in the wrong place. This can result in a more fearful puppy that will shy away from you and toilet in more obscure places to escape your glare. You need to summon all your patience to clean up quietly and calmly without giving your puppy cause for concern.

Failure to teach bladder/bowel control

Many owners will continue to leave puppy training pads around the house for the times when they go out, preventing their puppy from learning bladder and bowel control. If you do the same, even the slightest filling of the bladder or bowels will prompt your puppy to go on his pad. Instead, you should encourage him to extend his capacity for bladder and bowel control, to fit in with your need to leave the house for longer periods.

Once you have reached the milestone of your puppy toileting outside, continue to reinforce this action positively while removing training pads and increasing the amount of time your puppy must wait to go out. You may suffer a period of regression, but be patient and eventually your puppy will get the message.

Medical conditions

There are a number of medical conditions that can cause a puppy to suffer an inability to learn housetraining. Take your puppy to be examined by your vet to ensure that the toileting problems endured are not associated with any illness or physical abnormality.

▲ A well-housetrained puppy will tell you when he needs to go outside, often by scratching at the door.

Change in routine

Simply staying at work longer or asking friends to look after your previously well-housetrained puppy can result in a regression into toileting accidents. These are to be expected and some changes in routine need to occur so that your puppy can learn from his mistakes

PREVENTION

Train your puppy

You can follow the housetraining procedures outlined on pages 46–49, to establish the basis for a reliably housetrained puppy from the outset. You should be taking your puppy outside to toilet from his very first day at home.

CURE

Revamp your regime

Completely overhaul your routine at home with regimented feeding times for your puppy and regular-as-clockwork access to outdoors. You will have to fully commit to the time and effort this involves. Be extra lavish with your praise whenever your puppy goes to the toilet in the right place.

Stop all punishment

Over-punishment in the past must be replaced with calm, rational behaviour on your part. Find different, positive ways to channel your anger, such as in a vigorous form of exercise. Use hand clapping to interrupt inappropriate toileting indoors, then transport your puppy to your chosen location and give him lots of positive attention when he has finished going there.

Signpost with urine

Wipe the cleaning cloth that you have used to clean up urine indoors over a position outdoors where you would like your puppy to go, such as in a corner of your garden or near a tree in your local park. The scent of his urine should help stimulate your puppy's desire to urinate near the chosen spot, which hopefully should herald a switch to a pattern of toileting outdoors.

Grass marks the spot

Unlike many surfaces in your home, grass has a texture that is unique. Therefore, your puppy will be able to determine that grass is different from anything that he might find indoors (such as

▼ Transferring your puppy's urine scent outdoors may prompt him to toilet in the correct place.

carpet). The unique texture of grass enables you to give your puppy a clear indication that it is acceptable for him to toilet there.

Clean up wisely

With his ultra-sensitive nose, your puppy will be able to pick up his scent in areas where he has previously toileted even after the offending material has been removed. Major cleaning must be undertaken to remove not only the urine or faeces, but also the scent. Many home-cleaning products simply mask odours, so hot biological washing solutions or odour eliminators need to be used to avoid your puppy from toileting in the same spot. Sealing cracks in flooring and replacing grouting with waterproof material can also help to avoid stimulating scent accumulating, while keeping your home clean and hygienic.

Nervousness and fear

Being **ill at ease** around strangers, **hanging back** from meeting visitors and **hiding** behind his owner at the slightest **traffic noise** are not behavioural traits in a puppy that will grow to appreciate all that the world has to offer. Although some dogs are born more **nervous** than others, you as an **understanding puppy parent** can draw upon the **strength of character** in your puppy to ensure a **carefree life** together.

WHY

Genetic predisposition

Certain breeds of dog are known to be more nervous than others. German Shepherd Dogs and Fox Terriers, for example, are two breeds that can suffer from nervous dispositions, although this can be overcome with understanding ownership from an early age.

Freeze, flight or fight

In a situation where your puppy may feel challenged or insecure, he will instinctively react by either freezing, running away or, if he cannot perform the first two, exhibit aggression. The fight response is rarely seen in a young puppy, who will usually respond nervously by freezing still in the hope that he will go unnoticed while the frightening stimulus passes. This is a natural behaviour and should be ignored as it is quickly replaced by investigative interest. Owners who force puppies into frightening or stressful situations may stimulate unwanted reactions, resulting in behavioural problems.

Poor socialization and habituation

If your puppy is not properly exposed to many different people, places, objects and experiences from a very early age, he can develop into a dog with a fear of anything unknown (see page 55).

Unwitting reinforcement

Your puppy will exhibit some degree of fear or nervousness during his normal development into adulthood. The difference between a puppy that develops into a confident mature dog and one that lives in a perpetual state of anxiety can be down to the response of his owner. Giving a nervous puppy reassurance with comforting words can affirm in his mind that he really does have something to be worried about. To your puppy, your comforting words will sound like praise, which is given when he does something right. Comforting your puppy when he is nervous will unfortunately make him even more fearful in any future encounters, as it will teach him that nervousness is the correct way to respond.

Poor judgement

Reprimanding your puppy when he cowers away from something or someone or exposing him to unruly dogs or frightening environments can lead to him developing an increasingly nervous disposition. Always keep in mind that your puppy is young and naive, and that you are completely in control of who and what he is exposed to. One bad decision resulting in a frightening experience can result in your impressionable young puppy being scared for life.

PREVENTION

Socialization and habituation

From as early as eight weeks of age, expose your puppy to as many different types of people and household items as possible. Puppies are very impressionable creatures in the early stages of life, and this trait should be taken advantage of. By bribing him with attention and treats to make any novel situation positive, you can nurture the development of your puppy into a calm and confident dog.

Help him to overcome his fear

Train yourself to neither coddle nor condemn your puppy for nervous behaviour, but instead give him the chance to overcome his fears on his own. Always assess a situation wisely before rushing in

▼ Socialize, socialize, socialize – the key to a puppy that is calm and confident with other dogs.

to comfort or reprimand your puppy. If he isn't in danger, then give him time to overcome his fears, which will be quickly replaced with a puppy's normal investigative interest. Remember that if you constantly comfort a puppy when he is nervous, you reinforce in his mind that he has something to be worried about. Be a strong, confident leader, remaining calm and impassive in the face of any potentially frightening situation. Your puppy will look to you for guidance, see that you are unaffected and will follow your lead and calm down.

CURE

Desensitization

A wealth of patience is needed to help a nervous puppy overcome his fears and become a more sociable and easy-going dog. Determine what causes your puppy to be nervous, whether it is strangers, other dogs or traffic, and endeavour to desensitize him to these stimuli.

Traffic

A degree of fearful respect for traffic is desirable, although a dog that barks or scurries away at the slightest traffic noise will not be a pleasure to walk in built-up areas, leading to difficulties later in life. Choose a quiet street with a low but steady traffic flow and sit down near by, allowing your puppy to keep a good distance from the road. Do not reprimand or comfort him if he shows a fearful response; simply talk to him in a soothing, constant tone in your normal speaking voice. Gradually bring him closer to the road's edge over successive weeks, not moving nearer until your puppy is calmly ignoring the passing traffic. Be prepared for this process to take some time and allocate periods to work with your puppy when you also will be feeling calm.

Strangers

If your puppy is nervous when strangers approach, begin by sitting in a living room, garden or local park where there are people walking by or congregating at a safe distance. Once he seems perfectly calm, allow strangers to greet him from a distance without talking to or looking at him. Ask them to advance slowly, then stop at a short distance away while offering a treat, giving the puppy time and space to assess the situation and decide whether to meet the person halfway or not. Talk to the strangers during this time in a calm manner, giving them advice on helping your puppy to overcome his nerves, but without giving your puppy undue attention.

Other dogs

Puppy parties should be heavily relied upon to help you and your puppy learn to socialize with other dogs (see page 38). If you are unable to attend one, invite friends and family with dogs that are known to be calm and well mannered to meet your puppy. Closely monitor the meeting without over-controlling the situation, again taking into account that initial nerves shown by your puppy may quickly be replaced by playful exuberance.

Dogs in the park should always be strictly monitored, as one bad experience could lead to fearful and antisocial tendencies developing in your puppy. Never feel embarrassed to ask other dog owners if their dog is sociable before allowing them to meet your puppy – no meeting at all is better than a frightening one.

Divert his attention

Good basic training is a perfect way of taking a dog's mind off a potentially fearful situation. If your puppy appears nervous, command him to 'sit', then offer him praise and attention for responding correctly. Initiate a game or give him a treat so that his attention is on you and he is ignoring whatever stimuli may have previously unnerved him.

◀ Choose a quiet location in which to gradually habituate your puppy to passing traffic.

▲ If your puppy is fearful, tell him to sit and reward him with praise when he responds to your command.

Alternative therapies

If your puppy suffers with a naturally nervous disposition, there are alternative treatments that may help to soothe them. Therapies include homeopathy and dog-appeasing pheromone (see also pages 152–157 for more on alternative practices used on dogs).

Homeopathy Pulsatilla, aconite, oat tincture, impatiens, aspen and larch have all been used by homeopathic vets to treat nervous canines. Vitamin B deficiency has also been linked with a nervous disposition. However, any medicinal supplements should always be discussed fully with your vet and used in conjunction with behavioural techniques. Best results will be achieved in your puppy when such medicines are used in combination with extra training, improving the bond between you and building up his confidence.

Dog-appeasing pheromone (DAP) A specific pheromone or scent hormone produced by the mammary tissue of the bitch helps to calm her puppies. This hormone has been synthetically reproduced in spray and diffuser form to have the same effect on a nervous dog. Invoking that sense of wellbeing experienced when snuggled up to mum, these products can be highly effective in calming a nervous puppy when he arrives at a new home. Generally available from your vet, dog-appeasing pheromone is an excellent product that can be used to keep your puppy contented and happy. It can also help in preventing dogs from urinating indoors (see page 127) and in reducing territorial aggression.

Travel sickness and car phobia

Confined to a tin box **hurtling** from side to side, **stopping** without warning, with **images flashing** past and a low **rumbling noise** from below – a **car journey** is understandably a **frightening** experience for a puppy. Some will be **sick** on their first few journeys, while others will **whine** and **shake with fear**, resulting in an **aversion** to car travel.

WHY

Motion sickness

Some puppies will suffer from motion sickness, as do some people. This condition is similar to sea sickness, and is caused by the sideways movement of fluids within your puppy's inner ear. The movement makes your puppy feel nauseous, resulting in him vomiting. This can be a transient problem or one that haunts your shared car journeys in the long term.

Fear

A puppy can be anxious when exposed to a vehicle for a number of reasons: lack of experience of car travel, a negative association with car trips, such as going to the veterinary clinic, being involved in a car accident or previous experience of travel sickness. Just being confined in a stationary car can evoke a fear response, which can result in excessive vocalization, salivation, panting or vomiting.

PREVENTION

Early acclimatization

In the first few weeks of ownership, a puppy should not be taken outside the confines of your home and garden unless it is absolutely necessary. However, during this time, it is nevertheless important to acclimatize him to your car. A puppy at this age is in the process of learning about the world around him and is most likely to take the new experience in his stride. If you wait until you are allowed to take him for walks, he may be less able to cope with a potentially frightening experience, especially since it is likely that the only car journeys he will have previously experienced will have resulted in him being at the end of a veterinarian's needle!

Brief excursions

Transport your puppy on short journeys from day one in the way that you mean to continue, such as in a pet carry container secured with a seat belt, in a travel cage in the car's rear compartment or with a harness fitted and attached to a seat belt in the front or back seat. If you allow him to travel on your lap when he is small, he will understandably be upset when he is confined and relegated to the rear of the car or back seat when he matures. Keep the car journeys very short and relaxed, offering him a treat when the trip is finished to end on a positive note. A daily car journey is ideal, to help foster his acceptance of car travel as part of his new life. Slowly increase the journeys in length and introduce the occasional interlude out of the car, off the ground and safe from unvaccinated dogs (such as at a friend's house who doesn't have a dog) at a suitable stopping point en route.

Drive considerately

Moderate your speed when driving, take any bends slowly and smoothly and avoid shouting or blowing the car horn. This will all help to keep the journey as calm and relaxing as possible for your puppy. Provide fresh air to keep your puppy comfortable, but don't allow him to put his head out of the window as this can lead to eye injuries. Avoid smoking, which can lead to nausea in your puppy.

CURE

Slow and steady

Gradually allow your puppy to be exposed to the car and car travel in controlled stages. Firstly, get him comfortable with being in the confines of a stationary car. Play games with your puppy in the car to make it a positive and fun place to be. For example, get him to climb in after you in pursuit of a toy or treat, then reward him with lots of praise. Once he seems happy to be in the car, restrain him in the carry container, cage or harness and give him treats or indeed his whole meal. If you wish, you could even feed him all his meals in the car for a few days in order to nurture a positive association with being in the car.

Once your puppy accepts being secured in the car, take him on very short trips, just to the end of the road and back, keeping him calm by talking to him in a constant, reassuring tone. Don't give him any attention in response to nervousness; only give him praise when he is sitting quietly without any signs of anxiety.

Make car travel fun

When he is old enough to go for walks, drive your puppy to the park so that he can enjoy a car journey and not have it always ending in a visit to the vet. After a short journey, take your puppy out of the car and play with him, then on return to your vehicle, offer him a treat. These simple actions will reinforce the association of car travel with pleasure. If you have a puppy who is vocal or over-excitable

▶ Your puppy will be happier in the car if you associate travelling with toys and treats.

in the car, make sure you exercise him well before returning to your vehicle and avoid giving him too much attention when you are driving so that he will settle quietly in the confines of his carry container, cage or harness.

Alternative therapies

Various homeopathic products, such as gelsemium, oat tincture, skullcap, hops, rosemary, lime blossom, passionflower, valerian, rock rose, impatiens, aspen and larch, can be used as a supplementary approach to the techniques described above to calm and soothe a fearful or nervous puppy (see page 133). Obtain a prescription from a professional homeopathic practitioner and administer for a week. If there is no noticeable improvement in the behaviour of your puppy in the car, a different homeopathic remedy can be tried.

Anti-anxiety drugs

Used only as a last resort, there are certain medications that a vet or specialist animal behaviourist may recommend to help an older puppy overcome an irrational car travel anxiety. All training methods should be completely exhausted before considering this treatment and further habituation is recommended in conjunction with administering them.

Sick as a dog
Health-care strategies

Puppies, like young children, can get very sick very quickly. Being able to detect the early warning signs of illness is invaluable for your puppy's wellbeing, as is the ability to deal with minor complaints and emergencies at home. There is no substitute for veterinary treatment, but you may find some of the complementary therapies detailed here worth exploring.

Early warning signs

Your puppy should be a generally **happy and energetic** soul, with an **eagerness to eat** and a **willingness to sleep**. Being a responsible owner requires a clear understanding of your puppy's health needs and the ability to **identify accurately** the **early warning signs** of illness, to ensure his **quick recovery**.

CHANGE IN BEHAVIOUR

The most common cause of owners taking their pets to the vet is a noticeable change in behaviour. Whether he is quieter than normal, having difficulty sleeping or just not his normal playful self, a change in behaviour in your puppy tends to be the most accurate indicator of ill health.

CHANGE IN APPETITE

Try sharpening his appetite

Going off his food is a common sign of oncoming illness in a puppy. If he doesn't seem interested in eating, cover the food and put it away for an hour or two. Returning the food at his next prescribed mealtime will give him enough time to have developed an appetite.

Avoid pandering to his whims

A fussy puppy will do his utmost to get treats and tasty food all the time and will refuse entire meals in protest at his current diet. Do not automatically supplement his meal with an alternative, as your puppy will forever dictate what you feed him based on whim. He is just like a child who won't eat his greens and you as a puppy parent do know best. If you stick to a good-quality diet and don't weaken, the likelihood is that he will eat it at the next mealtime. If he still doesn't eat, then it may be worth phoning your vet for guidance.

CHANGE IN TEMPERATURE

A shivering or panting puppy that feels overly warm to the touch will benefit from immediate veterinary advice or attention. Some owners may choose to keep a digital thermometer at home for their own use and for when their puppy's temperature is in question. As the temperature of a sharp-toothed puppy can only safely be taken rectally, you should receive training in the sterile and safe use of a thermometer by veterinary staff before trying this at home.

While a warm nose in a puppy is traditionally seen as a sign of ill health, the reality is that a puppy may have a cold nose yet still be suffering from a fever. The only true measure of a puppy's temperature is a thermometer. The average body temperature of a puppy is 38.1–39.2°C (100.5–102.5°F), with temperatures of 39.5°C (103.1°F) and over described as feverish.

Use the puppy health check (see page 23) to familiarize yourself with the characteristics of a healthy puppy. Being able to assess quickly your puppy's general health at home means that you will be able to provide pertinent information to your vet when needed to help deliver accurate treatment and a swift recovery.

◀ Lack of appetite in a puppy is often a sign of approaching illness.

Common puppy illnesses

Many relatively **minor health problems** can be **prevented** from developing if **warning signs** are picked up **early** and swiftly, using **simple treatment** at home. However, some will require investigation and **treatment** at the **veterinary clinic**, but your daily vigilance will again **pay dividends** in your puppy receiving **prompt attention**.

EAR PROBLEMS

Examining your puppy daily is key to preventing problems affecting the ears. Commonly occurring in floppy or large-eared dogs such as Bassets or Cocker Spaniels, ear problems tend to be caused by infection, parasites or foreign bodies. Regular cleaning with cotton wool and ear-cleaning preparations is highly effective in keeping wax levels to a minimum, which once accumulated can lead to infection or parasite infestation. Checking inside your puppy's ears daily after walks can prevent the need for painful removal of foreign bodies from the ear canal by your vet at a later stage.

EYE PROBLEMS

Injury and infection are the most likely causes of eye problems in a growing puppy. Keeping a regular check on your puppy's eyes is paramount to ensuring healthy vision as he grows. Conjunctivitis is the most common cause of ocular discharge in puppies, and infection or injury requires a prompt visit to your vet. Dark discharge from the eyes on a daily basis is normal and, like 'sleep' that accumulates in our eyes when waking in the morning, this can be cleaned away from your puppy's eyes with moist cotton wool.

MOUTH AND TEETH PROBLEMS

Many owners will be disturbed by a puppy's loss of baby (deciduous) teeth, which can occur from around three months of age. Bleeding gums can also result when he chews on his toys. However, both these symptoms are normal as the puppy's adult teeth grow through.

Checking your puppy's mouth regularly and training him to be comfortable with this examination is essential in keeping his oral cavity in pristine condition. Learning how to brush your puppy's teeth daily is an excellent way to ensure healthy

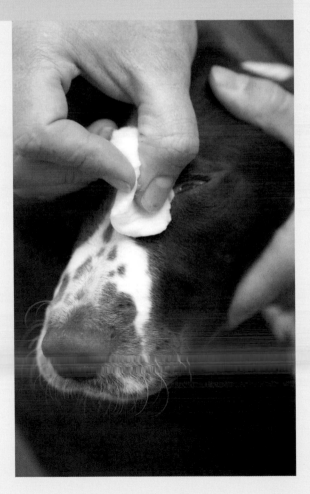

◀ 'Sleep' can be easily removed from your puppy's eyes using moist cotton wool.

◀ Check your puppy's ear canals daily for foreign bodies or signs of infection.

cause a puppy to be intensely itchy, resulting in alopecia developing most commonly over the ears, flanks, abdomen and tail. If not treated quickly, hair loss can worsen dramatically in a scratching puppy, with secondary infections being introduced to the damaged skin.

Preventative treatment

Home treatment with anti-parasitic medications prescribed by your vet should prevent the majority of skin irritations (see page 42), although if your puppy seems overly itchy or hair loss develops, make an appointment to see your vet.

COUGHING

Apart from a brief fit suffered after speedy consumption of food or water, a coughing puppy should always be taken to a vet for examination. Varying greatly in cause, coughs can be dry or wet in nature, productive or non-productive, or associated with ocular (eye), oral (mouth) or nasal discharges. Coughing can be caused by infections, foreign bodies or injury to or abnormal function of the lungs or heart, and accurate diagnosis is required to treat it effectively.

Kennel cough

This is one disease commonly known to cause coughing in young puppies. Contracted from breeding establishments, pet stores, parks or other high-concentration dog areas, kennel cough is a viral disease that is highly contagious. It causes a dry 'smokers' type cough, and can be further complicated by infection of the bacterium *Bordetella bronchiseptica*, resulting in a purulent nasal discharge.

Kennel cough can be prevented by vaccination, and treated with anything from symptomatic preparations (cough syrup) to specific antibiotic medications. The problem usually resolves around ten days after infection, although symptoms will be improved during that time by medication.

teeth and gums throughout his life. This also allows you to check your puppy's mouth in general, and to detect any problems that your vet should assess.

Warning signs

Signs that your puppy is unable to eat or is shying away from food require prompt investigation; fractured teeth due to chewing hard surfaces, foreign bodies, gum injury or infection are all conditions that need veterinary attention.

HAIR LOSS

Patches of hair loss (alopecia) that appear on your puppy should be closely monitored. Mites, fleas, allergy and bacterial or fungal infections can all

ANAEMIA

Diagnosed chiefly by pale gums, rapid breathing and weakness, anaemia is a lower than normal level of red blood cells in your puppy's vascular system. Mostly the result of high worm or flea burdens in a young puppy, anaemia can also be caused by bleeding wounds, poisons, toxins and immune reactions. If you suspect anaemia, the condition must be assessed immediately by your vet and treatment will almost certainly be needed to return your puppy to good health.

DIARRHOEA

Soft bowel motions are a common condition in puppies and should be monitored closely. A puppy suffering with diarrhoea lasting longer than one or two stools should be referred to your vet

▲ Bright pink gums are a sign of good health; pale or white gums could indicate anaemia.

immediately for treatment, since the condition can result in sudden dehydration. Diarrhoea is commonly caused by a change in diet or consuming rich or unsanitary food. A bright and otherwise healthy puppy can be monitored at home with food restriction for a few hours and plenty of fresh water available.

If diarrhoea continues, or your puppy seems lethargic or blood is present in his faeces, a consultation with your vet is advisable to treat the problem swiftly. A parasitic or bacterial infection can cause severe diarrhoea, which can require your puppy to be hospitalized on a drip to correct dehydration, while treating the cause specifically.

CONSTIPATION

A puppy should normally pass a few bowel motions every day. Constipation is diagnosed when your puppy does not pass faecal material for an extended period, resulting in accumulation in the lower bowels and discomfort. This condition commonly occurs after a change in diet to a higher-fibre alternative and can be relieved by mineral oil supplements, such as paraffin/malt products or faecal-softening, bulk-forming agents at home, or a small enema preparation at your vet clinic. Prevention can be as simple as stimulating your puppy to drink more by softening any dry food with warm water.

URINARY DISORDERS

Occurring infrequently in puppies, urine infections can be detected by owners through a change in the colour or consistency of the urine. A puppy that passes urine more or less frequently than normal could be suffering from a urinary infection, irritation or abnormality, so seek advice from your vet. Familiarizing yourself with the colour and consistency of your puppy's urine may be a little unpleasant, but has been proven an accurate tool in diagnosing urinary problems quickly at home.

The most common cause of urinary disorder is a bacterial cystitis, which will cause your puppy to strain and produce cloudy urine. This should be treated specifically according to the diagnosis made by your vet and will quickly resolve once your puppy is prescribed a course of antibiotics.

VOMITING

The forceful projection of digested food or gut contents from the mouth is known as vomiting. Many owners confuse vomiting with the act of bringing up undigested food, which is known as regurgitation and is commonly observed in puppies. Regurgitation tends to be a physical response to over-eating, grass consumption or poor settling of food contents in the stomach. It differs from vomiting in that your puppy will suddenly bring up his stomach contents, then recommence eating with no lingering side effects.

Vomiting tends to be physiological in nature as a result of nausea and is an attempt by the body to rid itself of the cause. Your puppy will tend to be a little depressed after vomiting and will abstain from eating for a short period. Caused by the consumption of foreign bodies, rotting food or poisonous materials, metabolic disease, infection or other nausea-causing conditions, vomiting should always be discussed with your vet as it can quickly lead to dehydration.

▼ Adding warm water to a dry-food diet can help to relieve your puppy's constipation.

Nursing your sick puppy

Once your **vet** has **examined** your **sick puppy**, only in the most **severe cases** will it be necessary for him to be **kept** at the vet clinic. After being **sent home** with **medication and advice**, your unwell puppy will need lots of **tender loving care** and patience to help him **recover** as **quickly** as possible.

WHAT YOU CAN DO
Provide warmth and quiet
Place your unwell puppy in a warmer part of the house, away from doors and drafts. Your puppy will recover better in a quiet environment, so place him in his puppy crate or play pen lined with blankets and possibly a heat mat or hot-water bottle. Keep noise to a minimum and boisterous children and other pets away to give your puppy the chance to rest and recuperate.

Provide the right food and water
If your puppy is suffering from a poor appetite, your vet may suggest alternative foods to stimulate him to eat. Be careful not to change his diet too dramatically, as this may lead to diarrhoea and further complicate matters. Warming up food using hot water, thereby improving its smell, can be an effective way of stimulating appetite. Clean drinking water must be available at all times.

Administer medication with care
Listen to your vet's advice and always read the labels before giving medication to your sick puppy. Measure out the dosage of tablets or liquid oral medication before administering and place it down the throat or mix it with food according to your vet's recommendation. Creams, drops or ointments should be applied with the help of a family member or friend, and the area of treatment cleaned well before and after to avoid a build-up of debris.

For safety reasons, make sure you keep all puppy medication out of the reach of children and any animals in the house.

Give toilet help
As your puppy may be too weak to go to the toilet normally, his housetraining may have to take a backward step. At regular intervals pick up your puppy and take him to where you would like him to go. Afford him extra patience and time in his toileting while he is unwell.

Monitor his condition
Keep a very close eye on your puppy's progress, monitoring his eating, drinking and toileting habits to ensure that he is getting better. Keep your vet clinic's phone numbers to hand and call for advice if your puppy is not improving or his condition seems to be deteriorating.

◀ While your puppy is recuperating from illness, give him some peace and quiet by confining him in a crate.

Puppy first aid

The home can be a **treacherous** place for your unsuspecting yet inquisitive and **adventurous** young **puppy**, with many **dangers** lurking **indoors and out** to catch him unawares. **Accidents and injuries** need to be dealt with **quickly and effectively** by you, ensuring his immediate **safety** and **preventing** further **injury** until he arrives at the **veterinary clinic**.

▲ If your puppy is injured, use a towel or blanket to scoop him up and remove him from further danger.

IN AN EMERGENCY

Stay calm
First aid for your puppy can potentially save his life and is something that every responsible owner should learn. The number one rule is **don't panic!** Take a moment to collect yourself, act calmly and think things through rationally. Never give human medications to your puppy and avoid offering him food, as an empty stomach is advisable for a general anaesthetic, which may be needed on his arrival at the veterinary clinic.

Safety first
Think before you act, as your safety is as important as that of your puppy. If you act rashly and injure yourself, you could place your puppy further in peril, as you may be the only person in the vicinity able to help him. Injured puppies that are frightened and in pain may try to bite anyone who touches them, including their owner.

First, assess the situation, then remove him from immediate danger (for example, off the road) using a thick towel or blanket, which you should keep in the boot of your vehicle in case of emergencies. Failing that, you could use a jacket

or coat if you are wearing one. Contact your vet immediately. Keep your vet's phone number to hand, ideally programmed into your mobile phone, but make sure you know the name of the vet's practice in case you need to find the number. Always phone ahead, as vets are not fully resident at their clinics and may need to travel to help you. Staff at the clinic will be able to give you advice as to what immediate action you should take.

Basic examination
A quick examination of your puppy is extremely useful when describing to the vet clinic the injuries that he may have sustained. Again with your own safety in mind, attempt to check the gums (they should be pink) and breathing (normal, laboured or noisy?), then assess for pain, ability to walk (lameness) and any discharges present. This information can quickly pinpoint your puppy's injury or illness and allow your vet to provide you with appropriate first-aid measures.

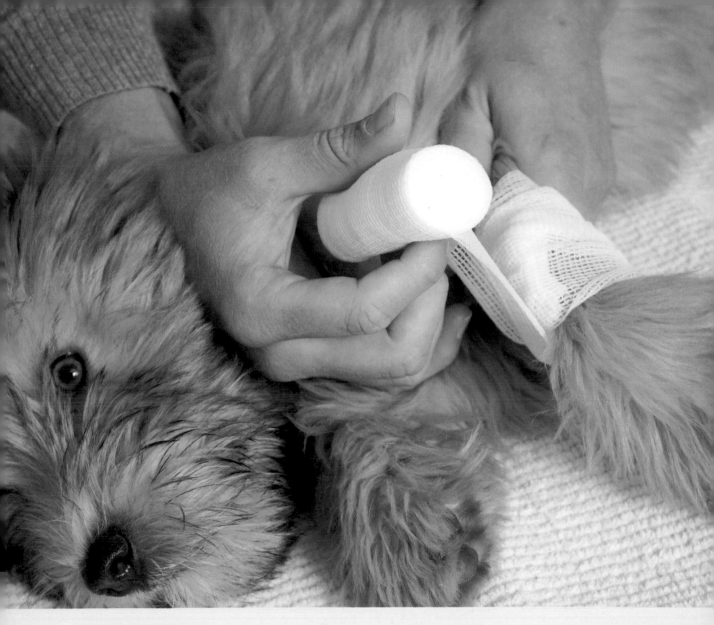

EXTERNAL BLEEDING

Caused by any number of injuries such as grazes, wounds or cuts, external bleeding is something that needs to be dealt with quickly. Apply pressure over the site with your hand or a bandage from your puppy first-aid kit (see page 151). If blood seeps through the first bandage, apply another one on top, as replacing the first bandage will remove the clot that has formed and bleeding will recommence. Don't apply a tourniquet unless bleeding seems to be unrelenting, as there is a danger of stopping circulation to the affected area, which may potentially result in gangrene. Do your best to keep your puppy as quiet and still as possible while you call your vet.

▲ Using a temporary dressing to apply pressure to a wound will help stem the bleeding.

Once the bleeding has stopped, clean the wound with warm, salty water. Don't use any household cleaners or human products.

INTERNAL BLEEDING

This can occur as a result of road traffic accidents (RTA) and symptoms can include: bleeding from the nose, mouth or rectum; coughing blood; blood in the urine; pale gums; collapse; rapid or weak pulse. If you suspect internal bleeding, keep your puppy as warm and quiet as possible during transit to your veterinary clinic.

BITE WOUNDS

Sustained by only the most unlucky of puppies, a bite wound is not only painful but can quickly become infected unless the treatment is swift. After you have applied pressure to control any bleeding, you should assess the wound by clearing fur away from the site using clippers or scissors. If the skin has not been punctured, the use of antiseptic cleaners may be all the treatment that is necessary. A full-thickness puncture wound of the skin will need more intensive treatment, with proper irrigation and a course of antibiotics prescribed by your vet to avoid infection.

BURNS AND SCALDS

Puppies do have a tendency to run under feet and scalds from hot drinks are periodically seen in the vet clinic. Burns caused by spitting coal or from jumping up onto hot surfaces can also occur. If this unfortunate fate befalls your puppy, take first-aid measures similar to those that you would use in the case of humans, such as applying a cold compress or immersion in water.

If your puppy is actually on fire, then the first action you take should obviously be to smother the flames immediately using a fire blanket, coat, rug or other suitable item. If you can, clean off whatever has caused the burn, such as oil or barbecue embers, then immerse the burnt area in cold water for approximately ten minutes. Remove anything that could constrict the site, such as a collar. However, you should leave the collar in place if it has been burned (unless it is causing breathing difficulties) to avoid causing any further damage to the puppy's burnt skin.

After you have bathed the affected area, keep your puppy warm and the wound covered with a saline-moistened dressing. You should avoid applying any topical creams or pain relief medication until you are able to seek veterinary advice and treatment.

▶ In case of burning, immerse the affected area in cold water for around ten minutes.

BREATHING DIFFICULTIES

Many situations may cause a puppy to have difficulty breathing and restrict his oxygen supply. Check his gum colour – a bluish hue indicates a severe respiratory emergency.

Drowning

This can occur when puppies are left unattended around water, such as pools, ponds and baths. If your puppy has swallowed a lot of water, first hold him upside down until all the water drains away. Only then can his lungs fill with life-giving air.

Choking

If you can see an object in the mouth, hold your puppy firmly in a towel and use a pair of forceps or something similar to remove it gently. Never pull something if it is lodged, especially swallowed string, which may concertina the intestines causing massive internal damage. If possible, take your puppy immediately to the vet.

Electric shock

Electrocution is the likely result of chewing power cables. Don't touch your puppy until the electricity has been turned off, using a dry, non-metallic item such as a broom handle to push him away from the power source. Consider giving artificial respiration if his breathing has stopped (see opposite) and call your vet.

Fits

If this uncommon event occurs, ensure your safety and the safety of your puppy by not trying to soothe or intervene until your puppy recovers. Move all furniture and electrical appliances out of the way, turn off any music and draw the blinds or curtains to create a calm, subdued environment. Some seizures will last for just a few seconds, but some can continue for minutes. Afterwards, your puppy will slowly regain consciousness, although he will remain recumbent and weak. Extend his neck to facilitate an open airway, loosen his collar and call the vet immediately.

RESUSCITATION

Expired Air Resuscitation (EAR) and Cardio-Pulmonary Resuscitation (CPR) are best left to the professionals, but if your puppy has stopped breathing and no help is available then you may need to come to his aid.

1 Lay the puppy on his side with his neck extended and his head slightly lower than the rest of his body. Check his airway for obstructions, clearing out any saliva or debris from his mouth with your hand (if your puppy is a victim of drowning, you should remove the water from his lungs by holding him upside down). Assess if the puppy is breathing by watching his abdomen, which should rise and fall, or place a piece of thread or grass in front of his nose to see if it moves. If there is no sign of breathing, you may need to resuscitate your puppy by using artificial respiration.

2 Close his mouth and, holding his nose with one hand while extending his neck, exhale a puff of air through his nose to expand his chest at a frequency of 15–20 times per minute.

3 Remove your mouth after each breath and check for signs of breathing. It is also important to check for a heart beat, either by gently squeezing over the heart to feel its beat directly or by checking for the femoral pulse. The heart can be located at around the point of the elbow in relation to the chest. The femoral artery is a large artery found on the inside of the back legs and is easily palpated in dogs for the assessment of pulse.

4 If you are certain there is no pulse, commence CPR. Firmly squeeze the chest at 15 compressions per 10 seconds (for an average-sized dog) to stimulate the heart to begin pumping again. Two breaths exhaled through the nose as in Step 2, should follow in quick succession. Repeat the cycle for one minute. Check again for breathing and pulse every minute. Once the puppy is breathing on his own, dry him off if he is wet and keep him warm. Seek professional assistance as soon as possible.

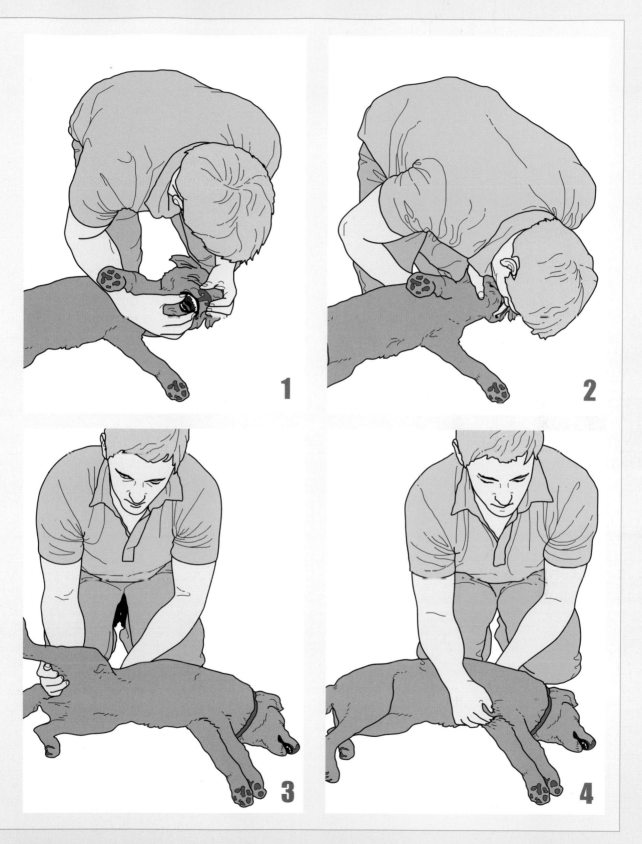

Warning You should use EAR and CPR only as a last resort, if professional help is not available, as the techniques can lead to injury of your puppy or yourself. These hints are not a substitute for professional assistance or proper study of first aid.

Insect stings and bites

An inquisitive puppy can easily suffer a painful bite or sting in the garden or park. If a sting can be seen, remove it below the bulbous poison sac using tweezers, then bathe the area with cool water or apply ice to soothe the pain. A solution of bicarbonate of soda for bee stings and vinegar for wasp stings are traditional remedies that are effective in neutralizing the poison. If a sting is present around the throat or mouth, visit your vet immediately as swelling may interfere with your puppy's ability to breathe.

▼ Establish why your puppy is limping by carefully checking the whole leg from top to bottom.

Snake or spider bites

If your puppy has been bitten by a venomous snake or spider, try to identify the culprit as best you can. Raise the affected limb or body part, pick your puppy up and convey him to the vet with speed for immediate treatment.

LAMENESS

When a puppy is seen limping, immediate assessment of the affected limb should be made. Gently check the whole leg from top to bottom for injuries, foreign bodies or deformities that may require veterinary attention. The worst example of lameness is due to broken bones. Falls or injuries indoors can lead to fractures, although the most

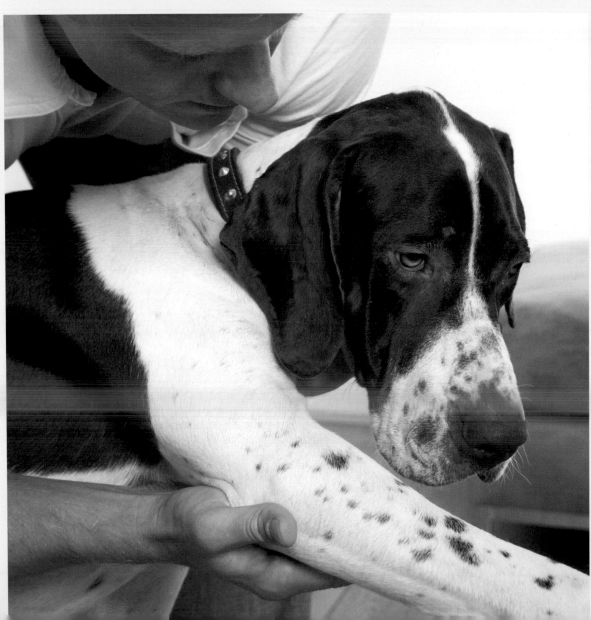

▲ If your puppy has a broken limb or other serious injury, wrap him securely in a towel to avoid biting or wriggling.

common cause of broken bones in dogs is road traffic accidents.

A broken bone can be detected by pain, swelling at the site, unnatural movement of the puppy's leg, deformity or a grating noise when touched. The most prudent first aid is minimal – only touch the fracture site if attempting to stem any bleeding. Pick your puppy up using a thick towel or blanket, with the injured leg uppermost, then place him in a padded carry container or box for transportation to your vet. Do not supply pain relief at home, but call your vet for advice before driving safely to the veterinary clinic.

TEMPERATURE EXTREMES

Your puppy can be very sensitive to changes in temperature and even limited exposure to extremes of hot and cold temperatures may cause him distress.

Hyperthermia

Commonly known as heat stroke, this potentially lethal condition is mainly seen when puppies are left in hot cars or unventilated rooms. Usually quite obvious to diagnose, symptoms of a puppy suffering from heat stroke include panting, excessive salivation and distress. The best treatment is immediate immersion in cool water or draping a wet towel around your puppy to lower his temperature. Offer him cold water to drink and monitor him closely while gaining further advice from your veterinary clinic.

Hypothermia

This is generally caused when a puppy is accidentally confined outdoors in winter and is unable to re-enter your home. A shivering puppy should be quickly dried off with towels, then warmed up slowly with multiple layers of blankets wrapped around him. Avoid attempting to warm up your puppy too quickly using hot-water bottles, as they may burn if applied directly to cold skin.

◀ Tasty but deadly: never allow your puppy to eat chocolate as it can be toxic to dogs.

Coat contamination

Poisoning can result if your puppy contaminates his coat by rubbing himself on a toxic substance, then begins to clean off the residue. Oil, grease or anti-freeze can be consumed in this way and are extremely dangerous. If such a substance has found its way onto your puppy's coat or paws, do not allow him to lick the area.

Wash the coat with soapy water or clip off the hair if the substance can't be removed. Never use turpentine or paint removers; washing-up liquid is a suitable product to apply. Always discuss potential toxic ingestion with your vet, watching your puppy closely to avoid further consumption of the contaminants during his journey to the vet.

Chocolate

A common cause of poisoning in puppies around Christmas or Easter is eating chocolate. Cocoa contains an ingredient called theobromine that makes chocolate toxic to dogs, causing vomiting, internal bleeding, seizures and even death. If you must give your puppy an Easter treat, purchase dog-safe chocolate drops from pet stores or supermarkets. Your puppy can eat these safely as they are theobromine-free.

Plants and trees

Some plants and trees are poisonous to dogs. Ask advice from your vet or garden centre to ensure that your home and garden are free from poisonous varieties. Plants that are poisonous to dogs include:

- aloe vera
- avocado
- cyclamen
- ferns
- hydrangea
- ivy
- lilies
- poinsettia
- yucca

POISONING

There are a surprising number of substances lurking in the home that are toxic to your puppy. The best treatment for poisoning is prevention – keep human medications in an inaccessible cupboard or cabinet, chocolate in the refrigerator or an out of reach cupboard and avoid cultivating poisonous plants or trees in the home and garden (see right). The common signs of poisoning can include vomiting, diarrhoea, nausea, drooling, seizures and dullness. Don't try to make your puppy sick, but allow him to drink plenty of water as he may try to make himself vomit. Common causes of poisoning include:

PUPPY FIRST-AID KIT

A first-aid kit is a necessity when owning a dog. It is best kept in a hard plastic container inside a convenient waist bag or backpack, as many injuries are sustained when your puppy is out on walks. The contents should include:

- ☐ white open-weave bandages of varying sizes
- ☐ adhesive bandages
- ☐ cotton wool
- ☐ swabs
- ☐ lint and gauze
- ☐ melanin (non-stick) wound dressings of varying sizes
- ☐ clean pieces of cotton sheeting
- ☐ small wash bottle containing saline solution
- ☐ tweezers
- ☐ round-ended scissors
- ☐ thermometer
- ☐ antiseptic cream or liquid
- ☐ mobile phone

▼ A simple first-aid kit for when you're on the go can be comfortably transported in a bag clipped around your waist.

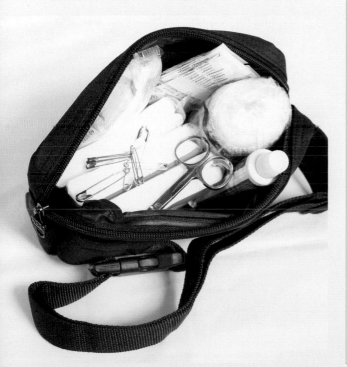

PUPPY EMERGENCY PLAN

Do

✔ Keep calm and use common sense

✔ Puppy proof your home and garden (see page 32)

✔ Study first aid further

✔ Have a first-aid kit to hand and keep it well stocked

✔ Keep your vet's emergency phone numbers accessible, for example programmed into your mobile phone.

Don't

✖ Panic

✖ Allow your puppy access to medicines, poisonous substances or rubbish

✖ Allow your puppy to chew small toys or anything that could be swallowed

✖ Ignore warning signs – contact your vet for advice if you are at all concerned about your puppy's wellbeing

✖ Be complacent – puppies can quickly get themselves into trouble by meeting aggressive dogs in the park, falling into water, straying onto roads or wandering outside in the cold.

Alternative medicines and therapies

Homeopathy and acupuncture are but the tip of the iceberg in this interesting New Age arena. Now you can take your puppy to **doga** (dog yoga) classes, then visit an **animal healer** to have his auras assessed. **Animal psychics** claim to be able to reach your puppy on a **spiritual level**, and with a dog's **hearing** around ten times the acuity of ours, only he will understand what **dog whisperers** are talking about. As long as no harm comes to the patient and no false promises are given, feel free to explore this field and, if nothing else, enjoy quality time with your puppy.

DOGA

How it works

Yoga, the ancient Indian Hindu practice now extremely popular as a low-impact human exercise, dates back to around 2500 BC. It is a combination of relaxation, breathing techniques and exercises that combats stress, helps circulation and improves core muscle strength and range of joint movement. Only recently has yoga been related to animals and it is thought to be a helpful means of calming and relaxing even the most highly strung dogs. Doga is now being practised all over the USA by yogis (people who do yoga) and their dogis (dogs who do yoga).

Popular doga poses

Designed to mimic many natural poses in canine behaviour, examples of yoga poses (*asanas*) used with dogs include: the triangle pose (*utthita trikonasana*), which looks very much like 'give paw' or 'shake' and requires three paws on the ground and one lifted, front or rear; the boat pose (*paripurna navasana*) or 'getting a tummy rub' pose, with your puppy on his back, which stretches the spine and tests abdominal strength; the pup's pose (*balasana*), the natural resting position for a dog, with his hind legs tucked up under him and his front legs outstretched.

ACUPUNCTURE

How it works

One of the most widely accepted forms of alternative treatment in Western medicine, acupuncture is a 2,000-year-old technique originally developed by the Chinese. Fine sterilized needles are inserted at specific points along the body's life-energy streams (*chi*), in order to correct their flow when disrupted by injury or disease. Acupuncture's primary action is via the central nervous system, and it is used to treat a variety of disorders – musculoskeletal, dermatological, reproductive, hormonal, gastrointestinal, respiratory and cardiovascular. Its main use in human and animal medicine is for relief of pain, such as that suffered during joint, bone, muscle or ligament injury.

Treatment

After initial sensitivity to the needles, acupuncture causes the release of endorphins, which are the body's natural painkillers, leading to a relaxed puppy who will occasionally fall asleep mid-treatment. Canine patients are treated in a home or clinical environment in approximately 40-minute sessions once or twice weekly for about six weeks. Specialist veterinary acupuncturists practise via vet referral, working to treat pain and other illnesses as an adjunct to conventional treatment.

The triangle pose – *utthita trikonasana*.

The boat pose – *paripurna navasana*.

BETTY'S DIARY
doga and me

Betty appreciated the time I spent with her rolling around in the park during our doga class and did seem to be calmer afterwards. Whether she was tired out with laughing at me trying to contort myself like human origami or felt the attainment of higher spiritual enlightenment, I'm not sure. She enjoyed the massaging and stretching, and the occasional treat that I used to trick her into the triangle pose.

As yoga tends to create a calming and soothing environment, all the dogis mirrored their masters' temperaments and were very chilled out. Betty was noticeably quieter than usual considering the number of strange dogs about. Some dogs joined in to howl when the chant of 'om' was used at the opening of the class. Often regarded as the original sound by Hindus, and a syllable with many meanings, it sounds not unlike a pack of wolves howling.

The classic downward-facing dog's pose used in yoga also appears in doga, as it replicates a dog's natural positioning. Other poses were a little less natural and some confused dogis pulled loose, preferring to sniff a nearby tree or each other. Our dogs had to be manipulated into certain poses, which in the hands of an over-zealous novice could lead to discomfort.

The pup's pose – *balasana*.

153

AROMATHERAPY

How it works

Experts in alternative medicine for animals believe that some essential oils, extracted from flowers, leaves, stems, roots, seeds and bark, not only improve wellbeing through the sense of smell but also have therapeutic uses in treating a number of canine conditions. From flatulence to motion sickness, bad breath (halitosis) to itchy skin, essential oils have been used to treat a long list of illnesses and infections in dogs.

Treatment

Aromatherapy should only be used after consultation with your vet regarding the specific condition. Essential oils must always be diluted with an oil base (such as olive oil) or a mixture of distilled water, glycerine and vodka, and never applied in pure form. As these medications are highly concentrated and your puppy has an acute sense of smell, they must be used sparingly, at around 25 per cent of an adult human dose. If you are interested in using aromatherapy to treat your puppy, consult your vet about contacting a respected alternative therapies practitioner in your area before beginning any home treatment.

HOMEOPATHY

How it works

Homeopathy was developed by Dr Samuel Hahnemann in the early 1800s in his Law of Similars. Based on the principle of exposing the body to agents (natural chemicals or toxins) that create symptoms similar to the disease needing treatment, homeopathy centres on the administration of minute doses of these agents to fight disease. An example of a homeopathic treatment used with canines is arsenicum-album, a diluted form of the poison arsenic, which would cause dullness, anxiety, thirst, jaundice and diarrhoea if consumed. When these symptoms are seen in a canine patient associated with another illness, the homeopathic dilution of arsenic is believed by homeopaths to stimulate the dog's vital force to react and begin healing.

Treatment

Using natural remedies, veterinary homeopaths attempt to reduce the amount of conventional medications administered to a canine patient, in the

▼ Aromatherapy can be used to calm a nervous canine, but consult your vet before attempting any treatment.

belief that this allows the immune system to respond naturally and overcome any illness suffered. Allergies, skin irritations and arthritis are all conditions that homeopaths claim they can treat, with homeopathic flea and tick control, vaccinations and diet also offered. Always discuss potential homeopathic remedies with your vet first and never stop giving the conventional medicines prescribed by your vet until both of the veterinary practitioners are in agreement.

HANDS-ON HEALING

How it works

A multitude of treatments and advice come under the banner of 'animal healing'. In hands-on healing, healing energy is channelled from the healer into the patient through touch and is used to treat a variety of canine ailments. Reiki is the most popular of the different types of hands-on healing advocated by alternative therapy experts to help improve a puppy's health and behaviour.

▲ Always give your conventional vet the opportunity to examine your pet before exploring alternative medicines.

Reiki

Originally practiced in Japan, the word 'reiki' comes from the Japanese words *rei*, meaning spirit, and *ki*, meaning energy. As well as being used by animal healers to promote general good health and wellbeing in dogs, reiki is also reported to release 'feel-good' endorphins in the canine patient, thus relieving any stress and promoting mental and physical relaxation.

Accessing therapy

When a canine patient cannot be approached by the reiki master, the practitioner can 'send' their treatment from a safe distance. If as a puppy owner you are interested in this therapy, bear in mind that reiki is not a substitute for conventional veterinary advice and treatment, and should only be undertaken with the knowledge of your vet.

◀ You can learn how to give your puppy a relaxing massage at home – he will enjoy it as much as we do!

MASSAGE AND PHYSIOTHERAPY
How it works
Specialist veterinary physiotherapists are working closely with a number of veterinary practices to speed recovery in dogs from accident and injury. Practitioners also teach owners massage techniques that they can use at home to help their dogs recover from training and exercise or to assist relaxation. These techniques are becoming more widespread, although permission from your vet should always be sought before consultation.

Treatment
Physiotherapists provide appropriate manipulation and massage techniques to help reduce pain, stimulate circulation and lymphatic drainage, relax muscles and increase joint mobility and range of motion in their canine patients. Pet insurance will often cover veterinary physiotherapy fees, as these techniques are proven to improve the recovery times of dogs suffering from injuries requiring rehabilitation.

MAGNET THERAPY
How it works
Used for human patients suffering from arthritic pain, this therapy has been adapted for use in dogs. Marketed to restore energy and relaxation, magnet therapy is also reported to enhance blood circulation, ward off parasites and have some anti-inflammatory action.

Treatment
Canine patients wear a collar or sleep on a bed containing 'reverse polarity' magnets to make them more comfortable and aid their recovery from injury or surgery. Magnetic dog collars are sold by some vets as an adjunct to anti-inflammatory medications for arthritic conditions, without any known side effects. This treatment is usually used alongside conventional therapy and should only be administered after consulting with your vet.

HYDROTHERAPY
How it works
Hydrotherapy is a non-weight-bearing form of exercise designed to rehabilitate dogs. The treatment is rapidly growing in popularity and gaining widespread support from the veterinary community. Hydrotherapy is ideal for dogs that are suffering from degenerative joint diseases such as arthritis or hip dysplasia and it is also very effective in fighting canine obesity.

Treatment
Participants are placed in a buoyant harness, then walked into a pool to swim by trained staff. High-powered underwater jets are used to create currents and a low-impact workout. In some cases, owners are able to share the experience and benefits with their pet. Sessions last for around 20 minutes and are relatively inexpensive – in some cases, the cost is covered by pet insurance. Ask your local veterinary surgery for advice on the closest facility.

DOG WHISPERING

How it works

A relatively new and increasingly popular technique, dog whispering is a version of dog training that incorporates some of the non-verbal training techniques used by horse whisperers to relate and interact with dogs. Dog whispering utilizes canine body language in conjunction with gentle actions and soft voice commands (different tones are used to differentiate between play and control times), thus avoiding anxiety or confusion in a learning puppy.

Treatment

Owners experiencing behavioural problems in their puppy can attend classes or one-to-one therapy sessions. This unique method of communication serves to create a special bond between owner and puppy, with positive reinforcement being used as a reward for desirable behaviours.

PSYCHICS

How they work

Animal psychics (or dog telepathists or animal communicators) claim to be able to help understand and correct canine behavioural difficulties, gain insight into health problems, determine your dog's likes and dislikes and even contact the spirit of deceased pets. These practitioners or mediums work with your dog's energies and use telepathic insight to get in touch with your pet.

Treatment

Sessions can help dogs to de-stress and prepare them for future changes of circumstance. Some psychics work over the phone without needing to lay an eye or finger on your pet to give their verdict on your dog's emotional state. Pet psychics are at heart animal lovers, with a calm and soothing approach. There is no harm in gaining these animal communicators' advice as long as you have consulted your vet. They use only non-invasive techniques that are, at the least, safe and fun. If no telepathic pearls of wisdom pass between you and your dog, just the attention and affection shared will not go unnoticed or unrewarded.

BETTY'S DIARY
living happily ever after

The first six months that Betty and I have spent together have been a true test of patience and a journey of enlightenment. Betty has grown into a happy and well-adjusted young dog who loves people and other dogs, and who is adorably sweet and well behaved both at home and around town. Obviously she still perpetrates the occasional misdemeanour, but as she continues to grow and mature she does more every day to make me proud and our love for each other is beyond all my hopes.

Puppy parenting is about wanting to do the best for your puppy. Now that you have made similar mistakes and learned from them in the same way as I have, I hope that your puppy becomes the happy, healthy and ever-loving dog of your dreams.

INDEX

ACKNOWLEDGEMENTS

Executive Editor Trevor Davies
Project Editor Fiona Robertson
Executive Art Editor Darren Southern
Designer Maggie Town, One2Six Creative
Senior Production Controller Martin Croshaw
Picture Research Jennifer Veall
Illustrations Peter Liddiard, Sudden Impact Media

Special photography:
© Octopus Publishing Group/Russell Sadur

Other photography:
Ardea/John Daniels 13, 42 bottom right
Corbis UK Ltd/George D. Lepp 12 centre right
Dr Scott Miller 83
Octopus Publishing Group Limited/Steve Gorton 23, 50–51 centre, 107 centre, 121; /Ray Moller 15 top left, 107 top right; /Angus Murray 14 top left, 14 centre right, 15 centre right, 15 bottom left, 16 top, 16 bottom, 17 top, 98, 106, 107 top left, 107 bottom right, 107 bottom left; /Russell Sadur 1–157, 21, 58, 60 top, 90 top, 154, 156 Science Photo Library/Eye of Science 41 centre; /Eric Grave 41 bottom

Author acknowledgements:
First and foremost I would like to thank my family, especially my parents, Muriel and John, for financing my university education and supporting my interest in becoming a vet and writer.

I'd like to thank everyone at Hamlyn, particularly Trevor Davies for giving me the opportunity to write this book and Fiona Robertson for making it look so fantastic.

A particular thank you to 'This Morning', especially Editor Anya Francis and Executive Producer Shu Richmond at ITV, for their support of my television journey from clinician to on-screen vet.

Thanks to my agent, Sue Ayton, for her initial introduction into the media and help in achieving my dreams. Also thank you to all my UK mates, clients and viewers who have supported me constantly through my time in the UK, my veterinary and TV career, and of course, in writing this book.

Finally I would like to thank Betty, whose exuberant exploration of the world, thirst for knowledge, enthusiasm and love of life every day act as a reminder of how we should all live our lives.